Are You Prepared to Teach Reading?

A Practical Tool for Self-Assessment

James Zarrillo

California State University, East Bay

PEARSON

Merrill
Prentice Hall

Upper Saddle River, New Jersey
Columbus, OH

Vice President and Executive Publisher: Jeffery W. Johnston
Executive Editor: Linda Ashe Bishop
Senior Editorial Assistant: Laura Weaver
Production Editor: Alexandrina Benedicto Wolf
Design Coordinator: Diane C.Lorenzo
Text Designer: Candace Rowley
Cover Designer: Kristina Holmes
Cover Image: SuperStock
Production Manager: Pamela D. Bennett
Director of Marketing: David Gessel
Senior Marketing Manager: Darcy Betts Prybella
Marketing Coordinator: Brian Mounts

This book was set in Times Roman by Integra. It was printed and bound by Command Web. The cover was printed by Phoenix Color Corp.

Pearson Prentice Hall™ is a trademark of Pearson Education, Inc.
Pearson® is a registered trademark of Pearson plc
Prentice Hall® is a registered trademark of Pearson Education, Inc.
Merrill® is a registered trademark of Pearson Education, Inc.

Pearson Education Ltd.
Pearson Education Singapore Pte. Ltd.
Pearson Education Canada, Ltd.
Pearson Education—Japan

Pearson Education Australia Pty. Limited
Pearson Education North Asia Ltd.
Pearson Educación de Mexico, S.A. de C.V.
Pearson Education Malaysia Pte. Ltd.

10 9 8 7 6 5 4 3 2
ISBN 0-13-222051-2

Brief Contents

Contents

Chapter 11   Literary Response and Analysis   65

Chapter 12   Student Independent Reading   71

Chapter 13   Supporting Reading Through Oral and Written Language Development   77

Teacher Preparation Classroom

See a demo at
www.prenhall.com/teacherprep/demo

Your Class. Their Careers. Our Future. Will your students be prepared?

We invite you to explore our new, innovative and engaging website and all that it has to offer you, your course, and tomorrow's educators! Organized around the major courses pre-service teachers take, the Teacher Preparation site provides media, student/teacher artifacts, strategies, research articles, and other resources to equip your students with the quality tools needed to excel in their courses and prepare them for their first classroom.

This ultimate on-line education resource is available at no cost, when packaged with a Merrill text, and will provide you and your students access to:

Online Video Library. More than 150 video clips—each tied to a course topic and framed by learning goals and Praxis-type questions—capture real teachers and students working in real classrooms, as well as in-depth interviews with both students and educators.

Student and Teacher Artifacts. More than 200 student and teacher classroom artifacts—each tied to a course topic and framed by learning goals and application questions—provide a wealth of materials and experiences to help make your study to become a professional teacher more concrete and hands-on.

Research Articles. Over 500 articles from ASCD's renowned journal *Educational Leadership*. The site also includes Research Navigator, a searchable database of additional educational journals.

Teaching Strategies. Over 500 strategies and lesson plans for you to use when you become a practicing professional.

Licensure and Career Tools. Resources devoted to helping you pass your licensure exam; learn standards, law, and public policies; plan a teaching portfolio; and succeed in your first year of teaching.

How to ORDER Teacher Prep for you and your students:

For students to receive a *Teacher Prep* Access Code with this text, instructors **must** provide a special value pack ISBN number on their textbook order form. To receive this special ISBN, please email **Merrill.marketing@pearsoned.com** and provide the following information:

- Name and Affiliation
- Author/Title/Edition of Merrill text

Upon ordering *Teacher Prep* for their students, instructors will be given a lifetime *Teacher Prep* Access Code.

This Book and the Teaching of Reading

This book reviews effective instructional practices for teaching reading in an elementary school classroom. It was written for teaching credential candidates who have completed, or who are enrolled in, reading methods courses. The book has two purposes:

- To help students prepare for an examination on reading instruction. Many states now mandate that all candidates for an elementary teaching credential pass some sort of "high-stakes, exit" test. This book should help you pass such a test.
- To help students review what they have learned about teaching reading. Most teacher preparation programs expose students to a great deal of information about reading methods from several sources, including comprehensive textbooks, methodology classes, and field experience. This book should help you remember what you have learned.

The text is "streamlined," containing essential information you should know before you take a test or begin teaching in your own classroom. This book is *not* a substitute for coursework or a more comprehensive methodology text on how to teach reading. The first chapter addresses planning, organizing, and managing an instructional program in reading. The second chapter covers some general topics related to the assessment of reading instruction. Chapters 3 to 14 cover the major topics in reading instruction (e.g., "Comprehension"), and each of these chapters provides important definitions, a selection of instructional strategies, and a summary of assessment options. Chapter 15 is a review of how to teach reading to English Learners, and Chapter 16 offers test-taking tips for those of you who face an end-of-program examination on reading instruction.

Acknowledgments

I would like to thank the following reviewers for their invaluable feedback: Diane D. Allen, Southeastern Louisiana University; Nancy Bertrand, Middle Tennessee State University; Ward A. Cockrum, Northern Arizona University; Randal L. Donelson, Ashland University; Karen Ford, Ball State University; Nancy Padak, Kent State University; and Timothy Shanahan, University of Illinois at Chicago.

CHAPTER 1

Planning, Organizing, and Managing Reading Instruction

INTRODUCTION

S-ABCD

This chapter describes the principles that should guide instruction at the *program* level. In other words, if someone were to observe a classroom over the entire school year, what consistent features would be present? The following five principles can help teachers plan, organize, and manage reading instruction:

1. Instruction is driven by local and state content **standards**.
2. Instruction is based on the results of ongoing **assessment**.
3. Instruction is **balanced**.
4. Instruction is **comprehensive** in scope.
5. Instruction is **differentiated** to fit the needs of all students.

To remember these principles, you might want to memorize the mnemonic **S-ABCD**. Successful teachers use these principles for their short-term and long-term instructional planning.

STANDARDS DRIVEN

Teachers should plan instruction with the following goal: Every student in the classroom will meet the content standards that have been adopted for your school. Although in some places standards are defined by the local school district, the trend nationally is for state departments of education to adopt standards that guide instruction in every school in the state. That instruction should be standards driven is an important point because too many beginning teachers either have no sense of the ultimate goal of reading instruction or, even worse, think that the goal is simply to move through a basal reader and accompanying workbook page by page.

Standards are statements of what every child is supposed to know and be able to do at each grade level. For example, first graders in California are supposed to be able to "distinguish long- and short-vowel sounds in orally stated single-syllable words (e.g., *bit/bite*)." The bottom line is simple: All of your instructional decisions, the materials you choose, how you group students, should be aimed at enabling every student in your room to achieve each of the standards for your grade level.

ONGOING ASSESSMENT

We will discuss this principle in greater detail in the next chapter. You should make instructional decisions on the basis of the results of ongoing assessment that utilizes a variety of assessment tools. For example, let us use the standard mentioned earlier. You want your first graders to hear the difference in long- and short-vowel sounds in single-syllable words (the difference between *bit/bite, bat/bait, bed/bead*). Ideally, you would test your students to determine who has achieved this standard and who has not. Those students who have met the standard will work on other reading activities while you provide direct instruction to those children who have not yet met the standard.

BALANCED INSTRUCTION

Daily, the children in your classroom should receive direct, explicit instruction in reading skills and strategies, *and* they should have opportunities to use those skills and strategies to read a variety of texts and write in several formats. This combination of skills/strategies lessons and actual reading and writing activities creates a balanced instructional program.

A *skill* is something that a reader does automatically (or with *automaticity*). The ability to decode is a skill; for example, knowing that the *c* in *cake* is "hard" and makes the /k/ sound, whereas the *c* in *city* is "soft" and makes the /s/ sound. A *strategy* is something a reader consciously chooses to implement. For example, a reader may want to get an overview of a chapter in a social studies textbook, so the reader previews the chapter by reading the first paragraph, all the subtitles, and the chapter summary.

Recently, there has been an emphasis on the importance of *systematic, direct,* and *explicit* skill and strategy instruction. There are two dimensions of *systematic* teaching. First, the teacher knows precisely what skills and strategies each student at each grade level should master, as defined by the relevant set of content standards. Second, the teacher is "systematic" in that the results of assessments focus instructional planning—those students who are not acquiring a skill or strategy are grouped together for additional lessons. *Direct and explicit* skill and strategy lessons are teacher-directed, and though the teacher may use any of a number of resources, the objective of the lesson is to teach a specific reading skill or strategy. These lessons are best taught to small groups of students who share a common need. For example, a first-grade teacher plans and implements a series of three lessons for five children who are having difficulty understanding that in words with the CVCe pattern, the vowel is long (words like *bite* and *cake*). In Chapters 3–14, you will read about direct, explicit lessons for all the major areas of reading instruction.

Another approach to the teaching of skills and strategies is to teach them *indirectly, implicitly,* or in an *embedded* fashion. In this type of teaching, the skill or strategy is part of some reading activity, but it is not the primary focus. For example, a second-grade teacher reads aloud the picture book classic, *Make Way for Ducklings.*

The teacher's main objectives are to provide an enjoyable experience for her students, to introduce the children to this and other books by author/illustrator Robert McCloskey, and to use the book as a springboard for student-authored stories about animals. The teacher, however, takes ten minutes to point out the two different spellings for the long *a* sound in the title—the CVCe in *make* and the *ay* digraph in *way.* This was a small part of the activity; it was a valid "teachable moment"; and it is an example of embedded skills instruction.

To provide balance, in addition to direct, explicit skills and strategy lessons, the instructional program should include *many opportunities for students to read and write.* These activities challenge the students to do many things, such as reading books the teacher has selected, reading books they have selected themselves, reading social studies and science textbooks, reading plays through reader's theater, chanting poems and rhymes aloud, writing in journals, composing and sending emails to students in other countries, authoring original poems and stories, and discussing books and stories in small group formats. You will read more about these activities in Chapters 11, 12, and 13.

COMPREHENSIVE IN SCOPE

Teachers should not get bogged down on any one component of a comprehensive reading program. Unfortunately, this happens. For example, a first-grade teacher who does nothing but teach phonics and a fifth-grade teacher who does nothing but teach spelling have not provided appropriate reading instruction for their respective students.

A comprehensive reading program will include:

1. *Assessment*, using multiple measures and conducted on an ongoing basis.
2. The development of *word recognition* skills. This includes phonemic awareness; some concepts about print; phonics and other word identification strategies; and spelling instruction.
3. The development of reading *fluency*, the ability to read accurately at an appropriate rate and with appropriate expression.
4. The development of reading *comprehension*, which includes the abilities to understand the literal meaning of the text, to speculate and hypothesize during and after reading the text, and to evaluate the text.
5. The development of reading "meaning" *vocabulary*, knowing the meaning of words.
6. The development of lifelong *independent reading* habits and an appreciation of *quality literature.*
7. The development of efficient reading of *content-area texts*, which include social studies and science textbooks and reference materials like encyclopedias.
8. *Supporting reading through oral and written language development.* This includes an understanding of the relationships among reading, writing, and oral language, and an understanding of the structure of the English language (correct usage, sentence structure, capitalization, and punctuation).

DIFFERENTIATED INSTRUCTION

Because each child's needs are unique, teachers must differentiate instruction to meet individual differences. Assessment will inform the teacher of each child's strengths and weaknesses.

Instruction becomes differentiated when a teacher no longer relies solely on "whole group" lessons. Teachers should use a variety of grouping formats. Teachers will form *flexible* groups so children who share the need for a reading skill or strategy will be taught efficiently. Groups are flexible because they exist for a single purpose and will be disbanded as soon as the teacher has completed the lessons planned for the group.

For other lessons, especially to teach comprehension, children will be organized so that each group is composed of readers with the same instructional reading level. These are *homogeneous* groups because the children in each group have the same ability. Finally, some groups will be composed of children with different reading abilities (*heterogeneous* groups). For example, a group performing a reader's theater presentation may have students with several instructional reading levels; there can be roles that require different levels of reading proficiency.

Those students who are having particular difficulty will need *individualized instruction*. These one-on-one sessions can be provided by the classroom teacher, a reading specialist, or an adult volunteer who has received appropriate training.

Differentiated instructional programs that focus on our youngest readers are called *early intervention* programs. These programs try to address reading difficulties at the first possible opportunity. Many offer individualized instruction, like Reading Recovery, which features highly trained teachers working in one-to-one settings. Other programs provide intervention to children in small groups.

Differentiated instruction is essential because teachers should do what is necessary to ensure that all students achieve grade-level standards. The goal is to develop reading competence among all our students, including English learners and students with special needs.

SHORT-TERM AND LONG-TERM PLANNING

Teachers should be able to incorporate the S-ABCD principles in both their short-term and long-term planning. Long-term planning is for the school year, often in two- or three-week "chunks." Short-term planning is for a single lesson or a series of a few lessons. Successful short-term and long-term planning requires each of the following:

- The teacher's thorough understanding of the relevant content standards. For long-term planning, the teacher should allocate enough time so that the full range of standards will be covered. In short-term planning, teachers should know precisely what standards are addressed in each lesson.
- A long-term plan that formally **assesses** students at regular intervals; short-term plans that provide for less formal assessment on an ongoing basis. The data from these assessments drive all instructional planning.
- Instructional plans that provide a program that is **balanced** in that it incorporates systematic, direct, and explicit teaching of skills and strategies, and many opportunities for students to use those skills and strategies as they read a variety of texts and write in many formats. Long-term and short-term plans should reflect a commitment to a program that is **comprehensive** in scope, allowing students to develop in all areas of reading and language arts.
- Long-term and short-term plans that meet the needs of all students, of English learners, speakers of nonmainstream English, and students with special needs. Your goal is to have an instructional program that allows each child to achieve to her or his full ability. Long-term and short-term plans will **differentiate** instruction by utilizing many types of instructional groups and providing individualized interventions.

All of this will require the prudent use of instructional resources. Most public elementary schools in the United States have adopted a basal reading series (e.g., Open Court or Houghton Mifflin). Each comes with many components. School and district-level resource centers provide other materials. Classroom, school, and public libraries should be used. Computer resources, including software and Web sites, have much to offer. The key to successful planning is to remember that the goal of instruction is to teach the standards; only those resources that help accomplish that goal should be selected.

Finally, instructional planning, both long-term and short-term, should be the result of reflective practice. Teachers should assess their own teaching and the utility of each instructional resource, continue to use what works, and abandon what fails.

CHAPTER 2

Assessment of Reading Development

INTRODUCTION

Assessment is the process of gathering, interpreting, and using data. The assessment of reading development is complicated because there are so many aspects of reading that must be measured. Here I am using the broader word *assessment*, rather than *testing*. Although many aspects of reading development can be measured by tests, there are other ways of gathering information. In this chapter, we are concerned with the general principles of assessment, some terminology you should know, and informal reading inventories (IRIs). *You will read about specific assessment instruments and procedures for each of the major areas of reading development in Chapters 3–14.*

Here are the four key points to remember about the assessment of reading development:

Assessment Is Ongoing

Teachers should gather information about their students' reading performance throughout the school year. Most elementary school teachers have always done this, to some degree. On the other hand, in many classrooms, especially in high school and college, data are collected only at certain times, usually right before grades are due. The point is that valuable information is generated every day in classrooms. This is not to say, of course, that a teacher should collect information about every student, every day.

Assessment Is a Process That Uses Multiple Sources

Subsequent chapters of this book will describe several ways of assessing student reading development. Some of them will be *formal*—tests of some sort. Others will be *informal*—such as collecting written work students have completed, writing notes about students on a computer, or tape recording a discussion.

The point here is that teachers should *not* rely on *one* source of data to make judgments. For example, if you want to draw conclusions about a student's reading comprehension, you could (a) administer the reading passages from an IRI and ask literal comprehension questions, (b) use a CLOZE test to measure her ability to read content material, like a social studies textbook, (c) take notes on the student's performance during a discussion of a juvenile novel she has read, and (d) collect her written answers to inferential and evaluative questions you asked after she read a story from the basal reader.

Assessment Drives Instruction

After a teacher collects information from a variety of sources and analyzes it to determine a student's strengths or weaknesses, the teacher should use this knowledge to plan instruction. In the ideal classroom, all instructional decisions would be based on the results of thorough assessment. Otherwise, teachers inevitably end up teaching some students skills and strategies they already know and teaching others skills and strategies that they cannot possibly learn because they do not have the prior knowledge to be successful or are not developmentally ready.

Assessment will determine how you *group* your students. Most of your groups will exist for a short time and will unite children who share a common need. For example, a kindergarten teacher has assessed her students' knowledge of concepts about print and determined that Joe, Lois, Leticia, and Thuy don't seem to understand the directionality of English (left to right, top to bottom). Those four students would meet with the teacher as a group to receive direct instruction on directionality.

Assessment will also determine the *resources* you use, the *teaching strategies* you select, and the *pace* at which you teach.

Assessment Is Standards-Based

Almost all public elementary schools in the United States have standards-based instructional programs. The ultimate goal of assessment now is to determine to what extent each student has achieved each grade-level standard. For example, one of the reading standards for fourth grade in California is that the student will be able to "distinguish and interpret words with multiple meanings." All fourth-grade teachers must assess each of their students to determine who has (and who has not) met this standard.

BASIC CONCEPTS AND TERMS

Reliability.   A test is reliable if the results of the test yield consistent scores across administrations. In other words, if you were to take Form A of a test on April 1 and Form B on April 2, your scores would be considered reliable if they are almost identical.

Validity.   A test is valid if it measures what it claims to measure. Let's take a moment to think further about this testing concept. Validity is a significant issue in the assessment of reading development. You might think that all scores on reading tests developed by professional test makers are valid. You might think that these scores always give you an accurate picture of what your students can and cannot do. This is not the case. Consider a typical standardized assessment of reading comprehension. Students are scored on their answers to questions that appear at the end of reading selections. For some students, these scores could be invalid because they possess the background knowledge to answer the questions at the end of a selection *without* reading it. For example, students read a three-paragraph selection on ancient Egypt. The first question asks, "Why did the ancient Egyptians build pyramids?" If these students had studied ancient Egypt during the school year, they might be able to answer the question even if they had not read the selection! Also, many reading comprehension tests developed long ago present reading selections that do not resemble the type of texts young children normally read now. Almost all stories our first graders read, for example, are illustrated. Until a few years ago, however, virtually all reading comprehension tests administered to first graders did *not* include stories with illustrations.

Standardized.   A standardized test is one that has an established, nonvarying procedure. Standardized tests have a manual for the person who administers the test, a script for the person to read. The tests have strict instructions and time limits. You have taken many tests like this—the person administering the test reads aloud something like, "Open your test booklet to page 5. Read the instructions silently. Begin working when I say, 'Start.' Continue until you reach the last item on page 12. Do not go on to page 13. You have 43 minutes. Start."

Norm-Referenced. Norm-referenced scores allow for comparisons between the students taking the tests and a national average. The makers of commercially published reading tests like the Stanford Achievement Tests (SAT) or the Comprehensive Tests of Basic Skills (CTBS) administer versions of the test to a sample of children. The result of this sample is used to create "norms," which are comparison scores. For example, a fourth grader taking a reading comprehension test gets 42 out of 60 questions correct; 42 is his "raw score." Is this good? Without norm-referenced scores you wouldn't know. If the average fourth grader in the sampling group scored 33, then our fourth grader scored above the average. He might well have a percentile score of 78 and a grade-level equivalent score of 6.3. Both tell us that he was reading above the national norm.

Percentile Scores. Percentile scores are norm-referenced scores. Staying with our example, a fourth grader who has a percentile score of 78 had a higher raw score than 78% of the sampling group. The higher the percentile score, the better. An "average" score would be 50. Someone with a percentile score of 15 has done poorly on the test, achieving a score higher than only 15% of the sampling group.

Grade-Equivalent Scores. Grade-equivalent scores are norm-referenced. A student's raw score is converted to a school grade level. Again, our fourth grader got 42 of 60 questions correct (his raw score). His percentile score probably would be around 78. It depends, of course, on how well the children in the sampling group did. His raw score is above average, so his grade-equivalent score would be something like 6.3. This means his performance corresponds to what a sixth grader in the third month of school would, on the average, achieve.

Stanine Scores. Stanine scores are norm-referenced. "Stanine" is short for "standard nine." Raw scores are converted to a nine-point scale. The number 5 is average, 9 is the top, and 1 is the bottom. Our fourth grader would have a stanine score of 8.

INFORMAL READING INVENTORIES

Once again, we will go over specific approaches to assessment for each of the major areas of reading development in the appropriate chapters. Now, though, we must review some information about informal reading inventories (IRIs). An IRI generates information about several aspects of reading development.

An IRI is a battery, or collection, of tests administered individually to students. For an IRI, one adult gives the tests to one student. No two IRIs have to contain the same collection of tests. The selection of tests for the IRI depends on the student's reading level. For example, an IRI for a sixth grader with average ability would *not* include tests of concepts about print, phonemic awareness, and phonics. An IRI for a first grader with average ability would. Here are the types of tests generally included in an IRI:

   Word recognition lists (described in this chapter)
   Graded reading passages (described in this chapter)
   Reading interest survey (described in Chapter 12)

Tests measuring concepts about print (described in Chapter 3)
Phonemic awareness test (described in Chapter 4)
Phonics tests (described in Chapter 5)
Tests of reading fluency (described in Chapter 6)
Structural analysis tests (described in Chapter 9)
Content reading CLOZE test (described in Chapter 10)
Vocabulary tests (described in Chapter 9)
Spelling tests (described in Chapter 7)

Word Recognition Lists

In this chapter, we will take a closer look at the word recognition lists and graded reading passages. The word recognition lists are sometimes called "graded word lists." These are lists of words, usually 10 in each list. There is a list for every reading level. The first list for kindergarteners is called the "preprimer" level, or "PP." It will have words like *the, am,* and *or*. The next list for kindergarteners, with slightly more difficult words, is at the "primer" level, "P." Then there is a list of words for every grade level from first grade to eighth grade. Some IRIs include word recognition lists for the high school grades, too. The words on the eighth-grade list will be difficult, like *psychology* and *endorsement*. The word recognition lists from one IRI, the *Bader Reading and Language Inventory* (3rd edition) are in Appendix A at the end of this book.

Children are asked to read aloud each word. The word recognition lists serve three purposes: (1) they provide a rough guess of the child's reading level so that whoever is administering the tests knows where to start on the graded reading passages; (2) the word recognition lists provide information on the child's "sight" vocabulary, the level of words the child can correctly identify; and (3) the child's performance gives information about his or her ability to use sound-symbol relationships (phonics) to decode words. The child's errors will provide a partial picture of what letters and letter combinations the child knows and which ones he or she needs to learn.

An example of a teacher's scoring sheet for a third grader's performance on the Bader Graded Word Lists is included as Appendix B. Different IRIs will have different instructions for administering the word recognition lists. Basically, students read the words and the teacher records the results, placing a check by words read correctly, noting which words are read with hesitation, and writing the word a child says when he or she misidentifies a word.

Graded Reading Passages

The most important part of the IRI is the graded reading passages. Like the word recognition lists, the graded reading passages are provided for every reading level from preprimer for kindergarteners to eighth grade. Some IRIs include graded reading passages for the high school grades. Since the graded reading passages can be used in a number of ways, an IRI usually includes two or more passages for each grade. An example of one of the first-grade passages from the *Bader Reading and Language Inventory* is included as Appendix C. A sixth-grade passage is Appendix D. Typically, the student is asked to read the passage aloud. After the student has finished reading, the teacher asks some comprehension questions or, with the youngest students, the teacher asks the child to retell what he or she has read.

Miscue Analysis. The word recognition lists determine which passage is first administered to the student. The student then reads the passage aloud, and the teacher keeps a detailed record of the student's performance. Though many teachers can record what the student says while the student is reading, it is easier to tape-record the child. The most popular form of this process, called a "Running Record," was developed in New Zealand. By looking at the student's errors we can gain a better understanding of how he or she reads. Patterns of errors will emerge and reveal how the child decodes print. Examining a record of a student's oral reading to identify and classify errors is called a *miscue analysis*. Each commercially published IRI has a different system for teachers to use to record the child's oral reading performance on the graded reading passages. One system is included as Appendix E. A scoring sheet for one child's oral reading is Appendix F. Oral reading errors fall into three categories.

Semantic Errors. These are meaning-related errors, like reading *dad* for *father*. The student has relied too much on the semantic cueing system and hasn't used graphophonemic clues. A child who repeatedly makes semantic errors understands what he or she is reading, but needs to be taught to use phonics skills to be sure that every word read makes sense from a graphophonemic sense (phonics is covered in Chapter 5).

Graphophonemic Errors. *Graphophonemic* comes from the Greek words for *symbol* and *sound*. These are errors related to the sound-symbol relationships for English, like reading *feather* for *father*. The words sound alike, but *feather* wouldn't make sense in a sentence where the correct word is *father*. A child who repeatedly makes graphophonemic errors is either (a) reading word by word and depending too much on phonics to read each word or (b) reading a passage that is too difficult for him or her, doesn't understand what he or she is reading, and thus can only try to decode each word.

Children who are reading word by word need to be taught to speed up (see Chapter 6). Children who don't use the meaning of the sentences and paragraphs to decode words need to be taught to use what are called *contextual clues* (see Chapter 9).

Syntactic Errors. To a linguist, syntax is the way words are placed in order in sentences. A syntactic error would be reading *into* for *through*. Both are prepositions. Syntactic errors make sense in that the error is the same part of speech as the correct word. As with semantic errors, a child who repeatedly makes syntactic errors needs to pay more attention to phonics, the sounds English letters make.

Frustration, Instructional, and Independent Reading Levels

After the child has read the passage aloud, he or she is asked to answer some comprehension questions for the passage. The questions are included in the IRI examiner's manual. The teacher reads the questions and the child responds orally. An alternative for younger children in kindergarten, first grade, and second grade is for the teacher to ask the child to *retell* the story. The IRI provides a list of characters, places, and events in the passage the child should mention. This form of measuring comprehension, called a *retelling,* has been shown to work well. The administration of the graded reading passages of an IRI will allow the teacher to determine each child's frustration, instructional, and independent reading levels. *This information is essential for teachers to know.* Different IRIs use different formulas, but those listed below are fairly standard.

Independent Reading Level. Books and stories at this level can be read and understood by the child without assistance from the teacher. A student's independent reading level is the *highest* passage for which the student reads aloud 98% or more of the words correctly *and* answers 90% or more of the comprehension questions correctly.

Instructional Reading Level.   Material at this level can be read and understood by the student with help from the teacher. The student's reading textbook (basal reader) should be at this level. The social studies and science textbooks should be at this reading level. A student's instructional reading level is the highest passage for which the student reads aloud 90% or more of the words correctly *and* answers at least 60% of the comprehension questions correctly.

Frustration Reading Level.   Books at this level *cannot* be read and understood by the child, even with help. (The child can *listen* to the teacher or someone else read material at this level and understand it.) For a passage at this level, the child correctly reads aloud less than 90% of the words *or* does not answer 60% of the comprehension questions correctly.

Don't forget: To determine instructional and independent reading levels, you must know both (1) the percentage of words the child read aloud correctly *and* (2) the percentage of comprehension questions the child correctly answered.

The graded reading passages can also be used to determine the student's ability to comprehend what he or she has read silently. Then the teacher has the student read the passage silently. The teacher asks the comprehension questions after the child finishes reading.

CHAPTER 3

Concepts About Print

INTRODUCTION

What Are Concepts About Print?

Concepts about print are essential, basic principles about how letters, words, and sentences are represented in written language. These concepts vary from language to language; here, of course, we are concerned with English concepts about print. To learn how to read, children must acquire these concepts. They should be learned by the time the child leaves kindergarten. The actual phrase "concepts about print" was coined by the New Zealand educator Marie Clay, who developed a test of concepts about print. The concepts are:

Print Carries Meaning.   This is the most important concept. Children have acquired this concept when they know that words are used to transmit messages—stories in picture books, product names in advertisements, and labels on things like bathroom doors. It is possible to know this concept and *not* be able to read the printed words in the text. For example, many children who have been read to before they come to school will take a favorite picture book, sit down with it, and tell the story as they look at the pictures. These children cannot read every word on the page but they have acquired the concept that the printed words *are* the story. They know that while the illustrations in a picture book help tell the story, a reader must read the words that appear on each page.

Directionality of English and Tracking of Print.   Students have acquired the concept of directionality when they understand that words/symbols written in English are read left to right and top to bottom. Tracking is evidence that this concept has been learned, because the child is able to point to the next word that should be read. Children who have mastered this concept understand they must perform a *return sweep* at the end of each line of text, moving from the far right of one line to the far left of the next one. They also know that books are read from front to back.

Sentence, Word, and Letter Representation.   Again, this concept is *not* the ability to read words and sentences or identify letters. Rather, it is the knowledge of the *differences* among letters, words, and sentences. To fully acquire this concept children must know how many letters are in a word. A child who has acquired this concept knows *word boundaries*, that is, how many words there are in a line of text. Finally, children need to know where sentences end and begin, which requires recognition of end punctuation (., *!, ?*).

Book Orientation.   This is knowledge of where the cover of a book is, the difference between the author's name and the title, and where the story starts.

For our discussion, I will include *letter recognition* as a subtopic under concepts about print. It will be dealt with in a separate section at the end of this chapter.

Children Who Do Not Understand "Concepts About Print" Must Be Taught Them

Many children will acquire all the concepts about print without direct instruction, especially if their parents or someone else has spent a great deal of time reading to them at home. Other children will acquire concepts about print by taking part in classroom activities like listening to their teacher read aloud, through shared book experiences, and by dictating stories transcribed by an adult. It is important to note, however, that some children will not come to school with a knowledge of these concepts. Some children will not acquire them easily, through informal activities. Then, these concepts must be explicitly taught. Teachers should assess their students. Those who need help acquiring concepts about print should be taught them in a direct, explicit manner.

HOW TO ASSESS CONCEPTS ABOUT PRINT

Concepts About Print Test

Marie Clay from New Zealand developed the *Concepts About Print* test, which at one time was very popular in kindergarten classrooms in the United States. Now it seems that more and more teachers are relying on tests provided by the basal reading system their school district has adopted, like Open Court or Houghton Mifflin. To administer Clay's *Concepts About Print* test, the teacher uses one of two special books, *Sand* or *Stones*. The books have some pages with the print upside down, some words with the letters reversed, and some lines of print in odd configurations. The teacher asks the student to do things like point to the front of the book, identify where the teacher should start to read on a page, and recognize the beginning and ending of a word. The test measures book orientation, directionality, beginning and ending of a story, word sequence, and recognition of punctuation and capital letters.

Informal Assessment by the Teacher

It is relatively easy for classroom teachers to assess concepts about print by using (a) any picture book that has at least three or four lines of text displayed in conventional form on most pages and (b) paper and pencil. The teacher asks students to perform tasks and keeps a record of the results.

For example, to assess directionality and tracking of print, at the start of a new page the teacher would ask the child to point to where the teacher should start reading. The child should point to the first word on the first line of the text. Then, as the teacher reads slowly, the child would be asked to put his or her finger under each succeeding word to track the flow of the print. To assess word boundaries, the teacher could cover up all but one line of text and ask the child how many words are on that line. To assess whether or not a child understands that print carries meaning, a teacher can simply ask the child to write something. If the child writes letters, rather than squiggles or illustrations, then the child understand that in English, letters are used to convey written messages.

Teachers should also use *observation* of student behavior to measure acquisition of concepts about print. Some school districts have developed checklists for this purpose. The checklist, for example, might include the following: "book in appropriate position when reading," "demonstrates return sweep," "knows where to start reading on the page."

HOW TO TEACH CONCEPTS ABOUT PRINT

Implicit (Indirect) Teaching of Concepts About Print

Reading Aloud to Students.   Reading aloud will teach many children that print carries meaning. Reading aloud also will help children recognize the covers of books. If the teacher is reading aloud a standard-sized picture book to a class of 20 students, then the children will not be able to see each word of the text. This means reading aloud will not teach directionality or sentence, word, and letter representation. Teachers should read aloud to the students every day, select high-quality books, and read with enthusiasm and panache.

The Shared Book Experience.   With shared book experiences, teachers attempt to achieve with a group of children what has long been accomplished when an adult shares a picture book with one child. When an adult, typically a parent, sits and reads a book to and with a child, this is called *lap reading*, though unless the child is a relative, you do not actually let him or her sit in your lap. The shared book experience was named by New Zealand educator Don Holdaway. The goals of a shared book experience are to discover good books, to see that reading books is fun, and to teach concepts about print. The shared book experience is a particularly powerful activity because it has the potential to teach all of the concepts about print.

Teachers use *big books* for shared book experiences. Big books are just that, over-sized picture books measuring at least 15 × 23 inches. Many big books have been written with predictable phrases or words as a part of the text. *Predictable books* are ideal for shared book experiences. Familiar predictable books whose predictable plots or language patterns are popular include *The House That Jack Built* by Jenny Stow, *The Judge* by Harve Zemach, and *The Napping House* by Audrey Wood. A shared book experience usually has the following components:

1. Introduction (prereading)—Look at the cover and point out features of the book, such as the author's name, the illustrator's name, and the title page. Then ask, "What do you think this book will be about?" or some other predictive question.
2. The teacher then reads the story with full dramatic punch, maybe overdoing it a little. The children join in on the predictable text. The teacher may pause to encourage predictions or comments. If the teacher wants to stress directionality and tracking of print, he or she will point to every word while reading it.
3. A discussion occurs before, during, or after the text reading. Children ask questions or talk about favorite parts or characters.
4. The story is then reread on subsequent days with the whole group, in smaller groups, with student pairs, or to individual students—acting out and enjoying the language patterns.

Language Experience Approach (LEA).   The LEA is intended to develop and support children's reading and writing abilities. Children share an experience such as a field trip to the zoo and then dictate an account of that experience to an adult, who records it verbatim. An LEA should record a personal experience that is vicarious and provides the child with a great deal to dictate. Together, the adult and child read the dictated text. The text is saved and bound in a child's personal reading book. Class experiences can be dictated by several children whose comments are collected on chart paper. The class then reads the dictated "story" together and the LEA is displayed in the classroom.

The LEA will teach most of the concepts about print. Repeated experiences will help children acquire the big idea—that print carries meaning. Teachers can have children follow along with their fingers as they read aloud. This will teach directionality and tracking of print. The LEA also is a good way to teach sentence, word, and letter representation. Portions of the dictated narrative can be reread, with emphasis on identifying sentences, words, and letters. The LEA, however, *cannot* be used to teach book orientation. LEA experiences also can be used to teach many other things like letter recognition, phonics, and vocabulary. After the teacher reads the dictated text, and the teacher and child read it together, any portion of the text can be used for a directed lesson.

Environmental Print. *Environmental print* refers to printed messages that people encounter in ordinary, daily living. This includes milk cartons, bumper stickers, candy wrappers, toy boxes, cereal boxes, billboards, menus, and T-shirts. Teachers should display examples of environmental print on bulletin boards and learning centers so children will see that print carries meaning. Lessons can be based on the letters, words, phrases, and sentences that appear on the items. Obviously, environmental print can't be used to teach book orientation, and it may not work for directionality because many product labels, advertisements, and T-shirts display words in atypical formats, with letters running over the surface in strange configurations.

Print-Rich Environment. All classrooms should be "print-rich," with plenty of examples of written language on display. For kindergarteners and first graders, this print-rich environment will help them acquire concepts about print. Children can then "read the room." There are many ways to create this environment:

- **Labels/Captions.** Classroom items should be labeled, like desks, chairs, the clock, and the windows. Bulletin board displays should have easy-to-read captions.
- **Morning Message.** The morning message is written on chart paper, in large letters, and provides an overview of the day's activities. For example, "Today is Wednesday, October 11. At 10 o'clock we will see a movie about farm animals. We will use fingerpaints to make pictures with the colors blue, yellow, and red." The teacher reads the morning message to the students and talks about the day and upcoming events. Students share news with the class. Sometimes, the teacher may wait to write the message until the children are seated in front of an easel with blank chart paper. Then the morning message provides an opportunity for children to see how words become print. The morning message can be used to teach directionality; letter, word, and sentence representation; and the concept that print carries meaning. The morning message, of course, cannot be used to teach book orientation.
- **Mailboxes.** Classroom mailboxes or "cubbies" can be made of milk cartons. They can be used to hold messages as students write to their classmates and the teacher writes to students (for many kindergarteners and first graders, the messages may have to be dictated and transcribed by an adult). Children discover the social purposes of language and that print carries meaning.

Explicit (Direct) Teaching of Concepts About Print

The previous activities will be enough for many children to acquire all the concepts about print they need. For others, you will need to plan direct lessons. For lessons on book orientation, you can use any picture book, assuming the children can see all the words. Big books are ideal for teaching book orientation to a larger group of children. For the other concepts about print, you can use any of the texts mentioned previously: picture books, environmental print, the child's dictated LEA narratives, or the morning message. The key is that in a direct, explicit lesson, you have as an objective one of the concepts about print. The concept won't be something children "just pick up" but do need to be taught specifically.

For example, for a child having difficulty with the directionality and tracking of English print, the teacher would select a picture book. First, the book would be read and enjoyed. Then, the teacher would return to the first page of the text and reread it with the child, guiding the child's finger underneath each word as it is read. For a lesson on word representation, the teacher could work with the morning message. In a direct lesson, children would listen to the teacher read a line and then chant and clap the number of words on the line.

Letter Recognition

Letter *recognition* refers to the ability to identify letters in both upper- and lowercase. Letter *production* is the ability to write the upper- and lowercase letters legibly. When talking about letter recognition, it is important to note that we are teaching the names of the letters, *not* the sounds letters make (covered in Chapter 5). Research shows that the ability of kindergarteners to identify letters is a strong predictor of future achievement in reading.

How to Assess Letter Recognition and Production.   Letter recognition is easy to assess. Simply display the letters randomly and ask the child to identify the target letter. The test is similar to an eye examination by an optometrist. The assessment of letter production requires two sources of data. First, a teacher should assess the child's ability to write the letters in isolation—the teacher calls out the name of the letter and the child writes it. The real test of letter production is whether the child can form each letter legibly when writing. This is an encoding in context task. Teachers would gather samples of student writing to judge the ability of each student to produce each letter.

Teachers should use a variety of multisensory methods to teach children the names of the letters: some that are visual, others that are auditory, tactile, and/or kinesthetic.

Associating Names and Things with Letters.   The teacher could display a large letter on the blackboard, like *J*, and then ask everybody whose name begins with *J* to stand underneath the *J*. Some teachers have 26 shoeboxes, each labeled with a different letter of the alphabet. Teachers then ask children to place toys or common classroom objects in the appropriate box, depending on the letter of the alphabet the object begins with. In the *B* box, for example, we would have books, balls, and a bandage.

Singing the Alphabet.   Many generations of children have sung the alphabet song. Remember, to teach the names of the letters, the song needs to be sung slowly as someone points to each letter. This is a good auditory experience.

ABC Books.   Teachers should read aloud books that are organized by the letters of the alphabet. There are dozens of these ABC books. Two of my favorites are *26 Letters and 99 Cents* by Tana Hoban and *Animalia* by Graeme Base.

Practice Writing Both Upper- and Lowercase Letters.   Children will learn the names of the letters as they practice writing them. These direct, explicit lessons should include clear instruction on how to make the letters and a reasonable amount of time for practice. Remember, kindergarteners are only five years old, and thus most have not developed the fine motor skills that allow them to write letters perfectly. This activity will help children who learn easily from visual experiences.

Tactile and Kinesthetic Methods. "Tactile" refers to touch. Tactile lessons include the use of concrete materials to practice the configurations of letters. For example, children could make three-dimensional letters out of modeling clay or trace their fingers over letters cut out of sandpaper. "Kinesthetic" refers to motion. Kinesthetic lessons ask children to make exaggerated movements with their hands and arms as they pretend to write letters that are 2 feet high in the air.

CHAPTER 4

Phonemic Awareness

INTRODUCTION

Phonemic Awareness, Phonological Awareness, and Phonics

Phonemic awareness is the ability to hear and manipulate the sounds of English. When a child can identify *duck* and *luck* as rhyming words or say that *duck* has three sounds and they are /d/, /u/, /k/, he or she is phonemically aware. Phonemic awareness can be taught without print. The development of phonemic awareness is an important goal for kindergarten teachers.

Phonological awareness is knowledge of the sounds in English. A child who has phonological awareness can identify and manipulate sounds in many different "levels" of language: (1) individual sounds, that is, phonemic awareness, and (2) sounds in larger units of language, like words and syllables. Phonological awareness is a broader term that includes the more specific phonemic awareness.

Phonics is knowledge of letter/sound correspondences, knowing, for example, that in the word *phonics* the letters *ph* make the /f/ sound. Phonics lessons must be taught with print (see Chapter 5).

Know the Phonemic Awareness Tasks

A student is phonemically aware if he or she is able to perform *all* of the following tasks. Some authorities on reading instruction use *phoneme* instead of *sound* in the descriptors (e.g., instead of *sound isolation*, refer to the task as *phoneme isolation*):

Sound Isolation. In this phonemic awareness task, the student must identify which sound occurs in the beginning, middle, or end of a word. For example, a teacher would ask, "What is the first sound you hear in the word *bottle*?" The correct answer would be, of course, /b/. Linguists, the people who study language, identify a single sound by putting a simple letter between slash marks, / /. This is because a single sound may have more than one spelling. For example, the *c* in *cat* and the *ck* in *duck* both make the sound /k/.

Sound Identity. The student must show that he or she recognizes the same sound when it appears in different words. The teacher would say, "*Time, tough, turn*. What sound is the same in each of these words?" The student should respond, "It is the first sound I hear, the /t/."

Sound Categorization. Here, the student is challenged to recognize a word that does not share the same beginning, middle, or ending sound as two other words. The teacher would say, "Listen carefully to these three words: *make, milk*, and *foot*. Which one doesn't belong?" The correct response is "*Foot* doesn't belong; the other two words start with /m/."

Sound Blending. The student must be able to manipulate individual sounds by combining them to form a word. The teacher says, "What word is made of these three sounds: /k/ (pause), /a/ (pause), /t/?" The student should respond, "*Cat.*"

Sound Substitution. In a sound substitution task, students should be able to substitute a sound every time a target sound appears in a phrase. For example, the teacher says, "Fe-fi-fiddly-i-o. Substitute *z*." The child would respond, "Ze-zi-ziddly-i-o."

Sound Deletion. In this task, the teacher says a word, then removes a sound and asks the students what the new word is. This works well with words with blends. The teacher says, "*Flag*, let's take away the *f*, and what do we have?" The student should say, "*Lag.*"

Sound Addition. This is the opposite of sound deletion. Here the student must identify the new word that is created when a sound is added to an existing word. The teacher says, "Listen to this word, *rat*. What is the new word we get if we add /b/ to the beginning of *rat*?" The correct response is "*brat.*"

Sound Segmentation. Sound segmentation is the most difficult phonemic awareness task. The teacher says a word and the child must identify each separate sound in the word. For example, the teacher says, "*Pop*. Tell me the sounds in *pop*." The correct answer would be /p/, /o/, /p/.

Research on Phonemic Awareness

Longitudinal studies of reading acquisition have demonstrated that the acquisition of phonemic awareness is highly predictive of success in learning to read. In fact, the level of a child's phonemic awareness in kindergarten correlates strongly with his or her level of reading achievement (word recognition and comprehension) at the end of first grade.

Why? Phonemic awareness is the *foundation* for understanding the sound/symbol relationships of English, which will be taught through phonics lessons.

Definitions

For both this chapter and the next ("Phonics and Other Word Identification Strategies"), you will need to know the following definitions.

The Alphabetic Principle. This principle is that speech sounds are represented by letters. English is an alphabetic language because symbols represent sounds. The sounds are called phonemes.

Phoneme. Most linguists would define a phoneme as a speech sound in a language that signals a difference in meaning: /v/ and /b/ are English phonemes because there is a difference between *vote* and *boat*. A simpler definition is: Phonemes are the smallest units of speech.

The Phonetic Alphabet and Graphemes. There are two ways to represent phonemes. *Phonetic alphabets* are created by linguists so that each phoneme is always represented by the same phonemic symbol. There is one-to-one correspondence between the phoneme and the phonemic symbol. For example, the phonemic symbol /e/ always represents the "long a" sound. This sound, /e/, can be represented by several graphemes, such as the *ay* in *say*, the *ei* in *neighborhood*, or the *ey* in *prey*. *Graphemes* are the English letter or letters that represent phonemes. Some graphemes are a single letter. For example, the phoneme /b/ in *bat* is represented by the grapheme *b*. Other graphemes consist of more than one letter. For example, the phoneme /k/ in *duck* is represented by the grapheme *ck*.

Vowels are sounds made when the air leaving your lungs is vibrated in the voice box and there is a clear passage from the voice box to your mouth. In English, the following letters always represent vowel sounds: *a, e, i, o, u*. Two letters sometimes represent vowel sounds: *y*, in words like *sky*, and *w*, in words like *cow*. Vowel sounds are said to be long when they "say their own name," as in *bake* and *bite*. Short vowels occur in words like *cat, pet, bit, cot, but*. R-controlled vowels are neither long nor short, as in the sounds *a* makes in *car*, *e* as in *her*, *i* as in *girl*, *u* as in *hurt*, and *o* as in *for*.

Consonants are speech sounds that occur when the airflow is obstructed in some way by your mouth, teeth, or lips.

Onsets and Rimes. Think syllable! Onsets and rimes occur in a single syllable. In a syllable, the onset is the initial consonant sound or consonant blend; the rime is the vowel sound and any consonants that follow. In the following chart, the onsets and rimes are represented by graphemes (rather than the phonemic symbols):

Syllable	*Onset*	*Rime*
Cats	c	ats
In	-	in
Spring	spr	ing

Remember: Onsets and rimes occur in syllables. All syllables must have a rime. A syllable may or may not have an onset. What would you say if someone asked you what the onset and rime was in the word *napkin*? You should answer, "Think syllable!" The onset in *nap* is *n*; the rime is *ap*. The onset in *kin* is *k*; the rime is *in*.

Phonograms are rimes that have the same spelling. Words that share the same phonogram are *word families*. Rime or phonogram: *at*. Word family: *cat, bat, sat*.

Blends are the combined sounds of two or three sounds. Examples of consonant blends are *pl* in play and *spr* in spring. Remember: The *bl* in *blend* is a blend!

Digraphs are combination of sounds that make a unique sound, unlike the sound made by any of the individual letters within the digraph. For example, *ph* in *phone* and *sh* in *share*. Don't forget: The *ph* in *digraph* is a digraph!

Diphthongs are glided sounds made by such vowel combinations as *oi* in *oil* and *oy* in *boy*. When pronouncing a diphthong, the tongue starts in one position and rapidly moves to another.

Beginning, medial, final refers to locations of phonemes. *Medial* means *middle*. *Cat*: beginning /k/, medial /a/, ending /t/.

HOW TO ASSESS PHONEMIC AWARENESS

In tests of phonemic awareness, the teacher talks, the student listens, and then the student says something. No print is involved. Older tests referred to these tests as *auditory discrimination*.

One widely used test is the *Yopp-Singer Test of Phoneme Segmentation*. In this test, the teacher says 22 words (for example, *dog, keep, fine, no*). The child must provide each sound of the word in order. So, when the teacher says *dog*, the correct response is /d/, /o/, /g/.

Remember, sound segmentation is the most difficult phonemic awareness task. So if a student does well on the Yopp-Singer Test of Phoneme Segmentation, you probably can assume he or she can do the other phonemic awareness tasks as well.

To do a complete job of assessing phoneme awareness, teachers should measure each child's proficiency in each of the tasks: sound identity, sound isolation, sound blending, sound categorization, sound deletion, sound addition, sound substitution, and sound segmentation. It is easy for teachers to develop simple assessments of these tasks. For example, to assess sound isolation, the teacher would actually create three tasks, one for identifying sounds in the beginning position, another for identifying medial sounds, and one for ending sounds. To assess medial sounds the teacher would need to create a list of 15–20 words with different medial sounds (which would be different vowel sounds, such as *bet, feet, cat, take,* etc.). For each word, the teacher would say, "Listen to me say this word, *feet. Feet. Feet.* What is the middle sound in *feet?*"

HOW TO TEACH PHONEMIC AWARENESS

For the teaching of phonemic awareness, we can distinguish *implicit* and *explicit* instructional activities. Implicit (also called "indirect" or "embedded") teaching refers to the use of books with rhymes and wordplay, chants, songs, and games. Phonemic awareness can be developed as a result of participating in lessons that focus on the sounds of words. Explicit, or direct, teaching refers to lessons with the stated objective of developing phonemic awareness. When children are first challenged with one of the phonemic awareness tasks, it is important that the teacher first *model* the performance he or she wishes the students to demonstrate.

Implicit (Indirect) Teaching of Phonemic Awareness

Books with Wordplay. These are books with texts that rhyme and/or feature alliteration (consonants) and assonance (a partial rhyme in which the stressed vowel sounds are alike but the consonant sounds are unalike: *late* and *make*). Examples: *Each Peach Pear Plum* by Ahlberg and Ahlberg and *I Can't Said the Ant* by Cameron. The teacher reads the book aloud and then asks questions or makes comments that focus on the phonemes in the text: "Did you notice how *cat* and *hat* rhyme?" Or, "This book is fun because of all the words that begin with the /*m*/ sound. Let's say them."

Rhyming Games. Children love to say words that rhyme. The goal is to have children chant rhyming words and then generate new rhyming words. The simplest type of game is to provide the first three rhyming words and then ask children to expand the list. For example, the teacher says, "*Pop, hop, top,*" and then asks for more words with the *op* rhyme. The children would say *mop, flop,* and so on.

Alliteration and Tongue Twisters. Again, alliteration occurs when two or more words begin with the same consonant sound. Tongue twisters usually are phrases with alliteration. Children love to chant these. There are many good books of tongue twisters, like *Faint Frogs Feeling Feverish and Other Terrifically Tantalizing Tongue Twisters* by Obligado.

Songs and Chants. Songs and chants that feature alliteration, rhyming, or assonance are good resources for building phonemic awareness. Simply choose a song or chant that focuses on the sounds of words, and sing and chant away!

Explicit (Direct) Teaching of Phonemic Awareness

Many children will come to school with phonemic awareness. Others will acquire it with little effort. For other children, however, acquiring phonemic awareness is a significant challenge. Kindergarten and first-grade teachers should assess their students to find out who is having difficulty with phonemic awareness tasks. For example, a kindergarten teacher has identified six children who have difficulty with sound isolation. They don't seem to hear middle sounds. The teacher should teach direct, explicit lessons on sound isolation to this group of six students. For these lessons, the teacher's objective is the development of the ability to isolate and identify middle sounds.

There are a number of points to remember about the direct teaching of phonemic awareness:

- Instructional activities focusing on the phonological awareness of larger units of language, like words and syllables, should take place before instruction in phonemic awareness. Some suggestions for teaching awareness of syllables and words are provided later in this chapter.
- It is better to focus on one or two phonemic awareness tasks at a time, rather than working on several of them simultaneously.
- It is a good idea to plan some phonemic awareness activities that involve the use of the letters of the alphabet. This helps children see the relationship between phonemic awareness and reading.
- Phonemic awareness instruction should be brief and not exceed 30 minutes for any one lesson. A review of the research showed that the most effective programs in phonemic awareness had less than 20 *total* hours of instruction. The amount of time devoted to phonemic awareness, however, will vary from child to child.

Direct teaching of phonemic awareness consists of lessons focusing on one or two of the tasks defined earlier: sound isolation, sound identity, sound categorization, sound blending, sound substitution, sound deletion, sound addition, and sound segmentation.

Sound Isolation.   In sound isolation, the children are given a word and asked to tell which sound occurs at the beginning, middle, or end of the word. The teacher could have a list of words that all have long vowels in the medial position: *cake, day, late, leap, feel, vote, coal, bite, like*. To model the desired response, at the beginning of the lesson the teacher would say each word and then say the medial sound ("*Leap, leap*, the middle sound is /e/."). At some point, the teacher just says the word and the children have to provide the medial sound. It is best to start with beginning sounds, then go to ending sounds, and then to medial sounds.

Sound Identity.   The teacher will needs sets of words that all share the same beginning, middle, or ending sound, but have no other shared sounds. For example: *lake, light*, and *low*. Those three words share only one sound, the beginning /l/. The teacher says each of the three words and then asks, "What sound is the same in each of these words?

Sound Categorization.   This type of lesson falls in the category of locating the "discrepant item," finding the anomaly among a class of words. Children are asked to find a word that does *not* share the same beginning, middle, or ending sound as two other words. This type of activity is easiest with beginning sounds, more difficult with ending and medial sounds. The teacher would say, "Please listen to these three words: *top, hip, hot.* Which one doesn't belong because it ends with a different sound than the other two?" The correct answer is *hot,* because the other two words end with /p/.

Sound Blending. In the simplest lessons to teach sound blending, the teacher says the sounds with only brief pauses in between each sound. The children then guess the word. Example: "Which word am I thinking of? Its sounds are /b/, /a/, and /t/." The answer would be *bat* or *tab.* The most difficult sound blending lessons challenge students to take "scrambled" sounds and rearrange them into words. For example, the teacher would say, "What word is made of these sounds, /a/, /t/, /b/?" Again, the answer would be *bat* or *tab.*

Another good way to teach sound blending is to ask children to blend an onset and a rime. For example, use the rime of *-ank.* The teacher would say /b/ and *-ank.* The children should say *bank.* Then, blend *th* with *-ank* and get *thank, cr* with *-ank* and get *crank.*

Sound Substitution. In this type of activity, the teacher asks children to substitute one sound for another. The hardest part of this for the teacher is finding phrases that work for this type of task. The easiest ones would be one-word substitutions. The teacher says, "*Cat, cat, cat.* Let's substitute the /b/ sound for the /k/ sound. We get *bat, bat, bat.*" Then the teacher might try simple alliterations (all start with the same consonant sounds). For example, the teacher says,"*Be, bo, ba, bu, bi*" (in this example of nonsense words, all the vowels are long). The students would then chant, "*Be, bo, ba, bu, bi.*" The teacher then says, "Let's substitute /k/ for the /b/. The students would then chant, "*ke, ko, ka, ku, ki.*" Obviously, it becomes more fun to do sound addition and substitution if you use a well-known chant from a song, like fe-fi-fiddly-i-o from "I've Been Working on the Railroad."

Sound Deletion. This activity works best with consonant blends. To avoid using nonsense words, identify words beginning with blends that will generate a new word if one sound is deleted. For example, *block,* take away the *b,* becomes *lock.* That works! *Frog,* take away the *f,* becomes *rog.* That doesn't work as well. In the lesson, the teacher says, "*Snail,* let's take away the *s,* and what do we have?" The student should say, "*Nail.*"

Sound Addition. Like sound deletion, this type of phonemic awareness activity works best with consonant blends. The same words used for sound deletion can be used for sound addition lessons. You could, for example, start with *lock* and ask, "What word do we build if we add the /b/ sound to *lock*?" The correct response is *block.*

Sound Segmentation. This is the most difficult of the phonemic awareness tasks. Children are challenged to isolate and identify the sounds in a spoken word. To teach this directly, the teacher should start with words with only two sounds. Remember, the teacher should always model the desired student behavior first. The teacher would say, "I am going to say a word and then slowly say the sounds in the word. *Bee.* (pause) /b/ (pause) /e/." Then the teacher would ask the students to say the sounds in two-sound words. After the children have shown they can segment two-sound words, lessons should focus on words with three sounds. The lesson challenges children to segment words with minimal differences, like *cap, cat,* and *cab.*

Teaching Phonological Awareness of Larger Units of Language

Word Awareness. The goal here is to help children become aware that sentences are made up of words. Lessons should start with activities utilizing monosyllabic, two-word, and three-word sentences. For example, the teacher has several cards, each with one word written on it. The teacher then builds two-word sentences (e.g., *Tom runs.*). The sentence is read as a whole, and then each word is read separately, with the teacher tapping the word card. Finally, a third word is added to the sentence (*Tom runs fast.*). A more challenging task involves the teacher saying a two-word, three-word, or four-word sentence and then asking the children to state how many words are in the sentence.

Syllable Awareness.   Syllable awareness will be more difficult for most children than word awareness because syllables, by themselves, are meaningless. Many children in kindergarten have no idea that they exist. A venerable instructional activity asks children to clap their hands as they say each syllable in a two-syllable or three-syllable word. Syllable awareness activities are easier if the teacher uses common words the children know and the pronunciation of the syllables is not distorted; they are uttered slowly and distinctly.

Word Blending.   In this task, the child is challenged to take two single-syllable words and combine them to make a compound word. Pictures can be used. The teacher would say, "This is a picture of a cow, and this is a picture of a boy. What do you get when you put *cow* and *boy* together?" The child should say, "*Cowboy.*"

Syllable Blending.   Here, children are required to blend two syllables into a word. The teacher would say, "What word do we get if we put *sis* and *ter* together?" The children, we hope, will say, "*Sister.*"

Onset and Rime Blending.   First, let's review the definition of *onset* and *rime*. You need to think at the syllable level. Onsets and rimes occur in syllables. In a syllable, the onset is the initial consonant (if any), and the rime is the vowel and whatever follows. In an onset and rime blending task, the teacher would say the onset, such as /b/, and the rime, *ank*. The children have to put them together and say *bank*.

Word Deletion.   In addition to blending activities, deletion tasks involving words, syllables, and onsets/rimes are appropriate for children who have difficulty manipulating individual sounds. In a word deletion task, the teacher says a compound word, identifies the two words that make the compound, and then asks the child to delete one of the words. The teacher would say, "*Kickball.* Listen carefully, this word is made up of *kick* and *ball.* *Kickball.* Now I want you to say *kickball* without the *ball.*" The child should say *kick*.

Syllable Deletion.   Likewise, a syllable deletion task requires the child to remove one syllable from a two-syllable word. The teacher would say, "*Playing.* The children are playing together. *Playing.* Please say *playing* without the *ing.*" The child should say *play*.

Onset and Rime Deletion.   The child must delete either the onset or the rime from a single-syllable word. The teacher says, "*Make.* Listen again, *make.* Now I want you to say *make* without the /m/." The child should say *ake*.

CHAPTER 5

Phonics and Other Word Identification Strategies

INTRODUCTION

Definitions

Word identification strategies are the "tools" readers use to recognize words. Word identification is the ability to read aloud, or decode, a word correctly. Please note that word identification does not mean knowing the word's meaning. Helping children expand their knowledge of word meanings is covered in Chapter 9, "Vocabulary." When children acquire efficient word identification skills, they can read with automaticity. That is, they do not get "bogged down" decoding words. They can focus their attention on understanding what they have read. Children can use the following word identification strategies to identify words:

Phonics. Phonics is the ability to make the correct association between the sounds and the symbols of a language. Using the Greek roots for *symbol* and *sound*, these are often called *graphophonic* relationships. Phonics is a set of many skills, such as the knowledge that the letter *c* makes both the /*k*/ sound (usually when the *c* is followed by *a, o,* or *u*) and the /*s*/ sound (usually when the *c* is followed by *e, i,* or *y*).

Morphology. To a linguist, morphology is the study of word formation. Children use morphological clues to identify words when they rely on root words, prefixes, and suffixes. Using these morphological clues is also called *structural analysis.* All lessons on morphology should involve teaching the meaning of root words, prefixes, and suffixes, so we will discuss the use of morphological clues to both identify and understand the meanings of words in Chapter 9.

Context Clues. In many instances, children can figure out an unknown word if they know the meanings of the words surrounding the unknown word. When children do this, they have used the context of the sentence or paragraph to identify the words. The use of context clues, which enable children to both identify and know the meaning of an unknown word, will be covered in Chapter 9.

Sight Words. Children should be taught to identify some words as whole units without breaking the word down by phonics or morphology. Two types of words should be taught as sight words: those with irregular spelling patterns and those that appear frequently in printed English (high-frequency words).

The Importance of Teaching Phonics Directly and Explicitly

In most school districts in the United States, these different word identification strategies are not of equal importance. Rather, in most schools the policy is that all primary grade teachers should teach children to identify words through phonics. Phonics instruction should have the following characteristics:

Instruction Should Be Systematic and Organized.   This means that teachers should have a clear list of the sound-symbol relationships students at their grade level should know. Students should be assessed to determine which sound-symbol relationships they have mastered and which they need to learn. Sound-symbol relationships should be taught in a sequence that moves from simple to complex linguistic units, starting with phonemes and then onsets and rimes, letter combinations, and syllables.

Instruction Should Be Direct and Explicit.   Some authorities in the field of reading instruction have been concerned that too many teachers appear to either teach phonics in a haphazard manner or not teach it at all. Although it is true that some children will acquire some sound-symbol relationships with seemingly little effort as they take part in such activities as shared book experiences and the Language Experience Approach, many children need to be taught phonics directly. In a direct, explicit lesson, the teacher's objective is to teach a sound-symbol relationship. These lessons are best taught to small groups of children who share the need to learn the same sound-symbol relationship.

HOW TO ASSESS PHONICS

To completely assess students in phonics, teachers should administer tests that ask students to (1) encode and decode in (2) isolation and in context. Many phonics tests are available. Most commercially published IRIs include phonics tests. Basal reading textbook series often include a set of phonics tests teachers can use. Teachers can develop their own "decode-in-isolation" phonics tests without much difficulty. The teacher simply needs to come up with a list of words that share the same sound-symbol relationship. Let's look at each type of phonics test.

Types of Phonics Tests

Decode in Isolation.   Decoding tasks ask the child to read aloud. In this type of test, the child is presented with a list of words and asked to read them. For example, if a teacher wanted to see which students know the sound of an *a* in the medial position in a one-syllable word, the test might consist of the following words: *mat, map, dad, pan, bad.* The teacher records what the child says for each word. If, for example, the child misidentified *mat* and substituted a long *e* sound, the teacher would write *meet* next to *mat.* Some IRIs include decode-in-isolation tests with nonsense words (*fap, fep, fup*). This provides a "control" on the test because the child must use phonics skills to figure out the word; he or she cannot rely on prior knowledge of the word as a sight word. A teacher should never rely solely on tests of nonsense words, however, because our goal is to see if children can understand the sound-symbol relationships in the words they will read every day.

Decode in Context.   This is the most important phonics test because it asks students to read part of a story or an informational article. Students read a passage of two or three paragraphs aloud. The teacher keeps a record of the child's miscues, looking for words that are misidentified. The teacher especially looks for sound-symbol patterns that are missed repeatedly (for example, a child missed *felt* and *belt*, two words that share the -elt rime). This type of test, as you remember, is done as part of an Informal Reading Inventory.

Encode in Isolation.   Encoding tasks ask children to write. The traditional spelling test is an encoding-in-isolation task. The teacher reads words aloud and the child writes them.

Encode in Context.   In this type of test the child writes a few sentences or a paragraph, and the teacher analyzes the child's writing to see which sound-symbol relationships have not been learned.

HOW TO TEACH PHONICS

Explicit (Direct) Teaching of Phonics

There are two general approaches to the explicit, direct teaching of phonics: *whole-to-part* (also called *analytic phonics*) and *part-to-whole* (also called *synthetic phonics*). Both approaches have supporters. Some basal reading textbook series feature whole-to-part lessons in their workbooks (Houghton Mifflin), while others rely heavily on part-to-whole lessons (Open Court). If you have a child who needs direct lessons in phonics, you should try one type of lesson and stay with it if it works. If the lessons aren't successful, try the other approach.

Whole-to-Part Lessons.   Whole-to-part lessons start with sentences and then "work back" to the sound-symbol relationship that is the focus of the lesson. Here is a lesson that teaches the *sh* digraph at the end of words:

1. Present a set of sentences on a piece of chart paper or on the blackboard, each sentence having a word with the common element. Underline the target word.

   My mom went to the bank and came home with a lot of <u>cash.</u>
   We went to the market and bought some <u>fish</u> and potatoes.
   I helped her <u>mash</u> the potatoes.
   After dinner, my brother Fred broke a <u>dish.</u>

2. Students read each sentence aloud with the teacher. Then the students read aloud the underlined word (*cash, fish, mash, dish*).
3. Then the teacher says, "There is something about the underlined words that is the same. What is it?" The children should note they all end with *sh*. If they don't, tell them.
4. The focus is now on the sound-symbol relationship. The teacher writes the letters *sh* on the board and, as the teacher points to the letters, the children make the appropriate sound.
5. The children then re-read the target words one more time.

Part-to-Whole Lessons.   Part-to-whole lessons begin with the sound and then build words. The teaching sequence would be:

1. The teacher writes the symbol on the board (*sh*) and tells children the sound that it makes.
2. The children say the target sound each time the teacher points to it.

3. The teacher shows letter combinations that can be added to the sound to make words. So the teacher would write *ca, fi, ma, di* on cards large enough for students to see them easily. The teacher places these cards in front of the *sh* written on the blackboard. The children would then blend the sounds to make a word (for example, *ca* and *sh* are read as *cash*).

Playing with Sounds, Letters, and Words: Word Sorts and Making Words

Word Sorts. Many teachers use word sorts to help children master phonics skills. During word sorts, children are provided with cards, each containing one written word. Word sorts can be simple or challenging; students can be asked to categorize (sort) words by sounds, spelling patterns, or meaning. For phonics, word sorts would ask children to sort a set of word cards according to a shared sound. For example, children could be given cards for the words *not, job, slow, fox, joke, load, top, hot,* and *post.* They would then sort the words into two groups—those with the short *o* sound and those with the long *o* sound.

Making Words. In this type of activity, the teacher selects a "secret word," which can be a child's name (*Angelina*), a word from a story (*duckling*), or a word relating to a seasonal event (*turkey*). Children are provided cards, each with one letter from the word on it (uppercase on one side and lowercase on the other). There will need to be several cards for each letter in the word, especially the vowels. The children are then challenged to make words from these letters using a pocket chart. For example, for *Angelina*, the children would see cards for *a, n, g, e, l,* and *i.* First, the teacher would ask them to make three-letter words (*nag, leg, gal*). Then they could be asked to add letters to make longer words (*angel, gain, nail*). Ultimately, children are led to the secret word (*Angelina*).

Implicit (Embedded or Indirect) Teaching of Phonics

The same activities teachers use to teach phonemic awareness and concepts about print can be used to indirectly teach phonics. The important thing, of course, is to help children learn the relationships between letters and the sounds they make.

The Shared Book Experience. With big books, children can see the words their teacher is reading aloud. Many shared book experiences end with an informal phonics lesson. The teacher might go back to a page that has rhyming words, point to the words, and have the children say them with him or her. Sometimes the words in a story can serve as the basis for a direct lesson. For example, after reading *The Cat in the Hat* by Dr. Seuss, the teacher may want to follow with a lesson on the *-at* rime.

Language Play with Rhymes and Chants. Rhymes and chants can be used to teach sound-symbol relationships. If the goal is to teach phonics rather than phonemic awareness, then the children must see the words they are chanting (remember, phonemic awareness is simply hearing the sounds). For example, to teach the *br* consonant blend, the teacher could write the following tongue twister on a piece of chart paper: "*Brilliant Brenda broke the brand-new brush.*" Read the twister aloud together (which is called *choral reading*). Then underline the *br*. Say the twister slowly and point to the *br* in each word.

Morning Message, Environmental Print, Children's Names, Things in the Room. All of these print sources can be used to teach phonics by simply calling attention to the sounds letters make. For example, the children might be challenged to make a list of all the things in the room that start with the /p/ sound (*pencils, people, paper,* etc.). The words are written on the board, and the target sound-symbol relationship is highlighted (in this case, the *p* at the beginning of each word is underlined).

SIGHT WORDS

Phonics is not the only word identification strategy students should use. In Chapter 9, we will discuss the use of contextual clues and the morphemic structure of words. In addition, however, every child should learn a large number of *sight words,* words that can be recognized instantly without reliance on some other word identification strategy. There are four sources of sight words:

1. High-frequency words that appear most frequently in the printed texts children read (*as, the, of*). Many available lists identify these "high-frequency" words, including Edward Fry's *New Instant Word List.*
2. Words with "irregular" spellings, like *dove* and *great.*
3. Words that children want to know, usually because they want to use them in their writing (*dinosaur, Burger King*).
4. Words that are introduced in content-area lessons in social studies and science (*insect, butterfly*).

It is easy **to assess** children's knowledge of sight words. Teachers should give children tests on sight words both in isolation and in context. In isolation, sight words are displayed to a child, either on flash cards or on a list, and the child reads them. It is important to determine if the child can read the words in context as well. When children read aloud from the graded passages in an IRI or from a story in a basal reader, and the teacher records the performance with a miscue analysis, the teacher can check to see which sight words were read correctly.

Teaching Sight Words

There are many ways **to teach** children sight words:

Word Banks.   A word bank is a child's personal collection of words that he or she knows well enough to recognize in isolation. The words are printed on small cards and kept in a small plastic bag or container. (It is best if the teacher writes the words.) Start with the child's name and other words that the child is likely to know (names of a pet, brother, the street where he or she lives). The teacher and the child then add words from each of the sources listed above: high-frequency words, words the child wants to know, and content-area words. When the word bank grows to about 100 words, it becomes unwieldy and should be translated into a personal dictionary in book form.

Word Walls.   Primary grade teachers use a variety of word walls to display words that the children are using in the classroom. Some word walls are large pieces of chart paper with a topic written in the middle (e.g., *Insects*) and related words written around the topic. Other word walls are alphabet charts with space above each letter for several words. During the first week of school the teacher adds the children's names to this word wall (*Andy* and *Abigail* go above the *A, Benito* and *Brittney* above the *B,* etc.). Then high-frequency and content-area words can be added.

Explicit (Direct) Teaching of Sight Words.   A whole-to-part approach to teaching sight words would go as follows:

1. First, select the words to be learned (*who, want, there, your*).
2. Then, write each word in a sentence, preferably in somewhat of a story format, with the target words underlined:

   "<u>Who</u> has my ball?" Matt asked. "I <u>want</u> it back."
   "<u>There</u> it is," Janet said. "<u>Your</u> coat is on top of it."

3. Next, read aloud the sentences, pointing to each word as it is read.
4. Then have the children read the story aloud with you.
5. Write each target word on the board, point to one word at a time, pronounce it, and ask the children to spell it and then say it.
6. As a follow-up, the words can be added to the children's word banks. The words can also be written on flash cards that can be used to review the words.

INTRODUCTION

The fluent reader reads swiftly and, seemingly, with little effort. Achieving fluency is important because without it, the nonfluent reader struggles to understand what he or she is reading. Indeed, there is a strong correlation between reading comprehension and reading fluency. During the past decade the importance of developing reading fluency has gained wide acceptance.

Components of Reading Fluency

There are three components of reading fluency:

Accuracy.   Fluent readers correctly decode the words they encounter in a text.

Rate.   Fluent readers read a text at an appropriate rate of speed, neither too fast nor too slow. There are really two components here: first, the ability to quickly decode *words*; second, to speedily read *phrases and sentences.*

Expression.   Fluent readers read with appropriate expression, varying their pitch (or intonation), stressing the correct syllables, and pausing and stopping when punctuation marks so dictate. Fluent readers are able to indicate appropriate "affect" in their reading, sounding surprised, sad, joyful, or excited. A sentence that is a question sounds like a question; a sentence that is an exclamation sounds like an exclamation. Rather than *expression*, this can be called reading with appropriate *prosody.*

Perhaps here it would be wise to distinguish *automaticity* and *fluency.* Automaticity refers to fast, effortless reading of words. Automaticity is the product of correct word identification (accuracy) and appropriate speed (rate). These are two parts, but not all, of fluency. Fluency also requires the reader to read with appropriate expression. It is not enough just to swiftly call the words out in robot-like fashion. Fluent readers are expressive.

HOW TO ASSESS FLUENCY

In order to assess fluency, teachers ask students to read aloud. This is an obvious point, but it bears repeating: Fluency can only be assessed through oral reading. Fluency has developmental aspects, especially in regard to rate. That is, what we expect of a first grader will be far different from what is acceptable for a sixth grader. Most veteran teachers know immediately when a child's oral reading has too many errors, or is too slow, or is too "flat" (without expression). More specific assessment in each component of fluency should be performed to verify these initial impressions and to identify the precise areas of need. Available, too, are a number of commercially published tests of oral reading (e.g., Gray Oral Reading Test, 4th edition [GORT-4], National Assessment of Educational Progress Fluency Scale).

Accuracy

To assess accuracy, teachers would follow the same procedures covered in Chapter 2, when I discussed Running Records and miscue analysis. The child reads a passage, and the teacher frequently tape records the child and then carefully analyzes the child's performance, noting each error. The target is 95% accuracy, the minimum required to place a passage at the student's independent reading level.

Rate

Assessment of reading rate requires the use of a watch. These are called "timed readings." Again, there are commercially produced test that can be used to assess reading rate. The excellent journal article by Hudson, Lane, and Pullen in the May 2005 issue of *The Reading Teacher* provides sources that offer appropriate reading rates for elementary school children. For example, by the end of first grade, students should read 40–60 correct words per minute. Fifth graders should read 118–128 words correctly per minute.

It is important to note that several factors will determine how fast a person reads. The easier the text, the faster anyone can read. Also, a reader's purpose will influence rate. Works of fiction, read for enjoyment, should be read much faster than a complicated cooking recipe, which must be read carefully.

Expression

It is far more difficult to assess expression, since there is a high level of subjectivity involved. During an oral reading, a teacher should listen for:

Appropriate Pitch.   The student's voice rises and falls at the appropriate times in a sentence.

Appropriate Response to Punctuation.   The student pauses for commas and semicolons, stops at the end of sentences, uses correct inflection for questions, and displays emotion while reading sentences with exclamation marks.

Appropriate Characterization.   When reading a story with dialogue, the child reader becomes an actor and sounds the way the character should sound.

HOW TO TEACH FLUENCY

Improved Word Identification Skills

Any student's reading fluency will improve when word identification skills improve. As students master the sound-symbol relationships of English (phonics), enhance their sight vocabulary, and learn how to use the structure of words to decode, they will read at a faster rate. Phonics and other word identification skills were covered in Chapter 5. It is important to note that word recognition lessons alone are not sufficient to improve fluency. The activities described here are essential.

Monitored Oral Reading with the Teacher

Fluency can be improved when the teacher works one-on-one with a student or with a small group of students. First, it is essential that students read texts that are reasonably easy for them—the text should be at the student's independent reading level. Remember, that means the student correctly decodes 95% of the words she or he will read. Also, the text should not be long, from 50 to 200 words, with the length of the text increasing for older children. A variety of types of texts should be selected, including stories and nonfiction. Poetry should be a frequent choice. Then two important activities need to take place in these fluency-focused lessons:

Teacher Model. It is important that children listen to models of fluent, efficient reading. During these lessons, the teacher should read the text aloud, modeling appropriate rate and expression.

Teacher Feedback. After listening to the teacher read the text, it is the student's turn to read aloud the same text. Being careful to avoid excessive interruptions, the teacher should respond to the student's effort. Sometimes the appropriate response is to select a phrase or sentence the child found difficult. The teacher would then model an appropriate reading of the phrase or sentence and the child would re-read. Other times, the teacher will note when a punctuation mark has been misread ("Be sure to stop when you see a period. Listen to me read the paragraph and listen for the three stops I make at the end of each sentence.").

These experiences, with the teacher working with one, two, or three children, are the best way to improve expression. Appropriate expression can only be taught through modeling and then guided practice. For example, the teacher might say, "Fred, the bear in the story is scared. When you read that sentence, you have to sound afraid. Listen to me . . . ."

Finally, the teacher needs to praise the student when he or she reads fluently. Success must be rewarded!

Repeated Readings

Repeated readings of the same text improve reading fluency. Again, the child should be reading a brief text at her or his independent reading level. The goal should be to have the student read the text four or five times. There are many formats for repeated readings.

Student Alone. Sometimes students should be told to re-read a text on their own that has been read aloud first by their teacher. This can be done in the classroom, or it can be a homework assignment.

Timed. In this form of repeated reading, the teacher selects a passage for the student at his or her *instructional* level (so it is more difficult than the texts normally used for repeated readings, which are at the student's *independent* level). The teacher then determines a challenging, but attainable, rate criterion. For example, "Sally, this passage has 150 words. I want you to read it in two minutes." Sally then reads and re-reads the passage until she hits the criterion.

Tape-Assisted Reading. This is a fluency activity that has been used for many years. It requires a recorded version of a text read aloud by a fluent reader. Note that not all recorded readings of a text are appropriate for tape-assisted reading. Those produced for listening alone are a valuable classroom resource, but they won't work for experiences where the student is expected to read along with the taped reader. There should be no sound effects, and it helps if the taped reader reads at a moderate rate, not too fast. Select a passage/tape at the student's independent reading level. The first time, the student follows along and points to each word in the text as it is read. During subsequent readings, the student reads aloud with the taped reader. Eventually, the student should be able to read the text fluently without the assistance of the tape.

With a Partner.   In this format, student partners take turns reading a text aloud. If the two readers have the same ability, then they simply alternate reading aloud. They might read aloud together. If one partner is more accomplished than the other, he or she should read aloud first, providing a model for the less fluent reader.

Reader's Theater

In a reader's theater presentation, the actors read their scripts. It is a popular form of drama in elementary school classrooms because the child-actors do not need to memorize their parts, there is minimal movement, and costumes and sets are optional. There are reader's theater scripts in most basal reading series, and it is relatively easy to adapt a picture book to reader's theater. Stories with a great deal of dialogue work best. Reader's theater provides an ideal opportunity for students to re-read a text.

Choral Reading

In choral reading, two more readers read aloud simultaneously. Poems, songs, chants, and tongue-twisters are the best types of texts for choral reading. The text is usually displayed on a piece of chart paper, with the words written large enough so that all children may see them. Some texts can be divided into parts, with different groups reading different parts. The teacher models appropriate reading of the text, and then the children read and re-read aloud together.

INTRODUCTION

It appears that a child's ability to spell is closely related to his or her word identification skills. Children who have mastered phonics skills—and know which letters are used to represent sounds—tend to be good spellers. Knowing how to spell also helps children expand their vocabularies and enhance their ability to write. One phrase that occurs frequently in discussions about spelling is *orthographic patterns*, which are the frequently occurring letter combinations of English spelling (e.g., the rime *-ight*, the suffix *-tion*). Elementary school teachers should know how to assess spelling development and use a variety of instructional strategies to teach children how to spell.

Finally, a word or two about "invented spelling." Many teachers have misunderstood this concept. Some authorities in the field have been concerned about teachers who viewed incorrect spelling as "no big deal." Invented spelling, of course, was never a goal of any sound instructional program. It is something that happens when young children who have not learned all the orthographic patterns of English begin writing. Teachers should encourage their students to take risks when they write—to use words they aren't sure how to spell. At the same time, every teacher's goal should be to move each child toward conventional spelling by helping him or her master the patterns of English spelling. Specifically, instruction needs to fit the stages of spelling development described in this chapter.

HOW TO ASSESS SPELLING DEVELOPMENT

Stages of Spelling Development

It is important that beginning teachers know how to analyze and interpret their students' writing to determine their level of development, and use that information to plan instruction. In our discussion we will use four stages of spelling development: prephonetic, phonetic, transitional, and conventional. It is essential to note, however, that as with any developmental stage theory, sometimes children don't fit neatly into these four categories. If a child is on the cusp of one of these stages, he or she might appear to be in two of the stages at the same time. Also, the jump from one stage to another doesn't occur overnight; children gradually move from one stage to another.

Knowing the child's level of development is important because it will tell you what type of instruction the child needs. Finally, your goal as a teacher is to move children through their current stage and on to the next stage. Your goal is not to bring all children immediately to the ultimate level of achievement—conventional spelling.

Pre-Phonetic.   Children at this level do not write at least one letter for each sound in a word; that is, some sounds in words are not represented. The child's first attempts to write typically reveal no understanding of the alphabetic principle. Words will be represented by letter-like scribbles initially until children begin to understand that words are represented by letters. Then, once a child knows that English writing means using our 26 letters, he or she will choose any convenient letter or combinations of letters to represent a word. *Cat* may be spelled *ABD.* Eventually, some of the sounds of the word are represented, but others are missing. *Banana* is spelled *baa.*

This stage is sometimes subdivided into the *precommunicative* and *semiphonetic* substages. Precommunicative spelling shows no understanding that letters represent sounds. If letters appear, they are randomly assigned. Semiphonetic spellers are aware of the alphabetic principle; they know that words are composed of letters. The child, however, does not have at least one letter to represent each sound. The child's writing is difficult, if not impossible, to read because many sounds in words are not represented. For example, a child wrote *aaLLo Sbav* to represent *my Dad's new car.*

Phonetic. Phonetic spellers know that letters represent sounds and at least one letter represents each sound in a word. The problem is, of course, that many times young spellers do not choose the right letter or combination of letters to represent sounds. To use linguistic terms, all phonemes have a grapheme. Writing at this level is somewhat difficult to read. For example, *I lik two flii a kitt* is *I like to fly a kite.*

Transitional. At this level, the child knows most of the orthographic patterns of English. All sounds have letters and for the most part, the child chooses the correct letter or combination of letters to represent sounds. Mistakes frequently occur with sounds that have several spellings, such as the long *a.* This is why the child writes *nayborhood.* Transitional spelling is easy to read. For example, *The firefiters have to be able to climb up the sides of bildings.*

Conventional. The child spells almost all words correctly. The only mistakes at this level occur when the child tries to spell new words with irregular spellings. Children at this level generally recognize that a word they have misspelled "doesn't look right." (This paragraph was, I hope, an example of conventional spelling!)

Methods of Assessing Spelling Development

In Isolation: The Spelling Test. The traditional spelling test, in which the teacher reads words aloud and the children write them, is one way of assessing spelling development. It asks children to encode words in isolation. The words included on the test, of course, should be words that the children have been introduced to and had a chance to study (more on the selection of words for study follows).

In Context: Writing Samples. Teachers should never rely solely on spelling tests to make judgments about the spelling development of their students. The real question is whether children will spell words correctly when they write. Teachers should collect and analyze samples of student work—their journals, their stories, their answers to questions. Look for patterns in the child's spelling choices. Which sound-symbol correspondence has the child clearly mastered? Which pattern is this child close to getting correct? For example, a teacher looks at the written work of a student who appears to think that the *c* only makes the *s* sound and is using a *k* when a *c* is called for (*kap* for *cap, kan* for *can*). This pattern of written behavior dictates that a series of lessons on *c* as *k* is in order.

HOW TO TEACH SPELLING

Selecting Spelling Words

Effective teachers know how to select appropriate words for their students to learn to spell. The traditional approach of providing a classroom of children with a list of 10 to 20 words to learn each week can be productive if (a) the words are appropriate, and (b) sound methods are used to teach children how to spell them. Also, teachers should differentiate the number of words children are expected to learn. A reasonable expectation for some children might be only four to five words per week.

It is essential that the words be appropriate for the children. Beware: A list of words that appears in a commercially published spelling book may or may not be right for any one group of students. What type of words should students be expected to learn?

1. Groups of words that have commonly occurring orthographic patterns: rimes, blends, digraphs, diphthongs, prefixes, suffixes, common root words.
2. High-frequency words, especially those that have irregular patterns. Lists of high-frequency words include the Fry New Instant Word List or the Dolch List.
3. Common-need words: Words that several children in the class have difficulty spelling correctly.
4. Content-area words: Words taken from social studies and science units of study.

Direct, Explicit Instruction of Orthographic Patterns

When the words share an orthographic pattern, the teacher should teach direct, explicit lessons focusing on that orthographic pattern. This is where spelling and phonics instruction come together. If the objective is to teach the -ate rime, the spelling list should have several words with that pattern, like *mate, fate, late, hate*. A series of lessons on this rime would include whole-to-part and part-to-whole instruction, reinforced by word sorts and making words activities.

Self-Study

Children should be taught how to engage in self-study of words they are learning to spell. It is a good idea to have a pretest so children know which words need to be given added attention. A simple method for self-study is the following sequence:

1. Look at the word and say it to yourself.
2. Say each letter in the word to yourself.
3. Close your eyes and spell the word to yourself.
4. Write the word and check your spelling.
5. Write the word again.

Multisensory Techniques

Teachers should use multisensory techniques to help children learn to spell. Some of our students will learn best from visual activities, while others will need either an oral or kinesthetic approach. The categories of multisensory techniques that teach spelling follow:

Visual. The simplest, visually oriented activity is for children to look at a word and then write it three or four times. Please note that having children write each spelling word an excessive number of times is not productive and, for some children, writing their spelling words multiple times does not help them. For others, it works.

Visual: Use of Color. For some of our students, the use of color makes an orthographic pattern clearer. For example, let us assume children are learning the *oa* digraph that appears in *boat* and *load.* Because some students are confusing the positions of the *o* and *a,* the teacher may have them write each word three times, using a blue crayon for *o* and a red crayon for *a.*

Auditory. Other students will learn to spell words with greater ease if they hear each letter of a word each time they write it. This results in a noisy study session, of course, but it can be beneficial. Instead of just writing each word, the child says each letter aloud as he or she writes it. In another approach with a "buddy," as one student writes, the other whispers each letter in his or her ear.

Kinesthetic. Kinesthetics is the science of human motion. Kinesthetic approaches to spelling include writing words in the air with large, exaggerated strokes.

Tactile. Tactile approaches are highly motivational and work best with our younger students. They involve touch. I have seen teachers use sandpaper, window screens, and shaving cream for tactile spelling activities. For example, with the window screens, each child writes each letter with his or her finger on the screen.

Mental Imagery. In this type of activity, the children close their eyes and pretend they see someone or something write each letter of a word. For example, a group of children are learning to spell *apricot.* Their teacher asks them to close their eyes and visualize the teacher writing *apricot* in blue ink on a whiteboard. The teacher says each letter in the word slowly as the students, with their eyes closed, create a mental image of the word being written.

Etymology and Morphology

Finally, teachers should select words that will facilitate direct lessons on the etymology and morphology of words. Etymology is the study of the origin and development of words. For example, fourth-grade students trying to learn how to spell *field* might be helped by a lesson on this word's origin. It is from the German word *feld.* The spellings of the two words can then be contrasted. Another example: A sixth-grade teacher could include the words *nutrition, nutrient,* and *nurse* on a spelling test. Their common origin is the Latin word *nutrire,* meaning *to nurture.*

Morphological lessons focus on prefixes, suffixes, and root words. See Chapter 9, "Vocabulary."

Small Group and Individualized Spelling Instruction

Spelling lessons and tests designed for an entire classroom must be used in conjunction with small group and individualized spelling instruction. The results of assessment—spelling tests and analysis of student writing—will reveal that some children share specific needs. These children should be placed in a small group and the teacher should provide direct, explicit instruction on the orthographic pattern they need to learn. Individual intervention in spelling can be very productive. Sometimes all that is required is a 10-minute lesson in a one-on-one setting to teach a child a bothersome pattern that the child repeatedly fails to spell correctly.

Stages of Spelling Development and Instruction

In the *pre-phonetic* stage, lessons should focus on concepts about print, phonemic awareness, and then on phonics. Children need to acquire the alphabetic principle before beginning to associate the correct symbol with a sound.

In the *phonetic* stage, the focus is on phonics—teaching children regular, frequently occurring sound-symbol correspondences. As the child moves through this stage, lessons should include rimes, prefixes, and suffixes.

When children are *transitional* spellers, lessons on the morphology and etymology of words will be helpful (e.g., a lesson on the common root, *graph*, meaning "writing"). Other lessons should reveal alternative spellings for the same sound, such as the many ways to make the long *a* sound (compare *bait, fate, hay, neighbor*).

Conventional spellers should expand their knowledge by learning highly irregular words and words for specific content areas. For example, during a unit on the solar system, students would learn how to spell *asteroid, satellite,* and *orbit.*

Spelling Instruction in Context

Students need opportunities to apply their spelling skills through writing experiences in several curricular areas, especially social studies and science. Spelling lists at every grade level should occasionally include words from the content areas. The key is providing children many opportunities to write essays, notes, and reports in social studies and science.

INTRODUCTION

Levels of Comprehension Skills

Comprehension refers to the reader's understanding of what is being read. Although there are many different taxonomies, or systems, that can be used to classify reading comprehension skills, we will use three: *literal*, *inferential*, and *evaluative*. Other taxonomies propose a different number of levels. Bloom's Taxonomy of Educational Objectives, for example, has six levels. This is important: Do not think of reading comprehension as one "thing." It is possible to be proficient in literal comprehension tasks and be lacking in inferential and/or evaluative comprehension.

Here are some examples of comprehension skills organized under these three levels:

1. Literal comprehension skills

   Identifying the main idea when it is explicitly stated
   Identifying important details
   Identifying the sequence of events in a story

2. Inferential comprehension skills

   Inferring the main idea when it is not explicitly stated
   Inferring cause-and-effect relationships
   Speculating on possible endings to a story
   Speculating on why a character has acted as he or she has

3. Evaluative comprehension skills

   Recognizing an author's bias
   Detecting propaganda
   Judging the quality of the author's writing

Comprehension Strategies

Comprehension strategies are things readers choose to do to help them understand what they are reading. Many are mental and are done in the reader's head (often called *meta-cognitive*), while others involve the use of pencil and paper. Teachers need to help their students become proficient in using these strategies.

Self-Monitoring. Good readers evaluate their comprehension of what they are reading and realize when they don't understand the text. Interestingly, less able readers rarely monitor their reading and do not alter their behavior when they don't understand what they are reading.

Re-Reading. This is called a "repair" strategy. A reader's self-monitoring should reveal when he or she doesn't understand a text. A good reader stops and does something. The most common repair strategy is to go back and re-read, usually to the previous paragraph or page. Other repair strategies include asking the teacher a question, looking up the meaning of a word in a dictionary, or taking a second look at an illustration.

Summarizing. Proficient readers can identify the main ideas of what they have read. They can retell a story or an essay in shortened form by highlighting the important elements of what they have read.

Note-Taking and Outlining. Note-taking and outlining are two techniques a reader could use to summarize and organize the important information in a text.

Mapping. Proficient readers can represent the significant events of a story, usually in a chronological format. To represent the structure of a story, readers can use story maps, story grammars, and story frames (all described in this chapter).

Literature Logs. Literature logs are a place for children to record their thoughts about what they have read and to generate questions, speculate, or summarize.

HOW TO ASSESS READING COMPREHENSION

The assessment of reading comprehension is multifaceted. Teachers need to (1) determine each child's independent, instructional, and frustration reading levels; (2) gather data on each child's mastery of comprehension skills at each level (literal, inferential, and evaluative); and (3) gather data on each child's mastery of reading comprehension strategies.

Determine Reading Levels

It is important that teachers know the independent, instructional, and frustration reading levels of every student in the classroom. This information reveals, in a general sense, which level of reading material each student can comprehend. Teachers should use the graded reading passages of an informal reading inventory (IRI) to gather this information. The use of graded reading passages on an IRI and the process of determining reading levels were described in Chapter 2, "Assessment of Reading Development." Remember, these reading levels are a function of (a) the percentage of words the child read aloud correctly and (b) the percentage of comprehension questions the child answered correctly.

After you have properly administered the graded reading passages of an IRI, you will know each student's instructional level. This is important, because most comprehension lessons should require the child to read texts at this level. There are two things that the results of this type of "placement" assessment do not reveal: (1) whether a student will be able to read a specific story or article, because the instructional level generated by an IRI is a rough estimate; and (2) which specific comprehension skills and strategies a child has mastered and which ones need to be developed.

Assess Comprehension Skills at Each Level: Literal, Inferential, Evaluative

Using Question-Answer Relationships (QARs).   All too often, teachers only assess literal comprehension. To be sure that all levels of comprehension are tested, the QAR system works well for a teacher-developed assessment. Taphy Raphael created the QAR system to teach reading comprehension. It can also be used to assess students' mastery of all levels of comprehension skills—literal, inferential, evaluative. The QAR system sorts questions into four categories on the basis of their relationship to where the answer to the question can be found.

Right There.   This type of question measures literal comprehension. The answer is easy to find in the text (i.e., the answer is "right there" on page 142, second paragraph, third sentence). The answer is in a single, identifiable sentence, such as this one from the first chapter of *Charlotte's Web* by E. B. White: "Why did Mr. Arable think he should kill Wilbur?" (Because he was the runt of the litter.)

Think and Search.   This is another type of literal comprehension question. The answer is in the text, but it is in two different parts of the text (the complete answer is not in a single sentence). Example: "How do we know that Fern loves Wilbur?" (On page 4, she says, "Oh, look at him! He's absolutely perfect." On page 7, she can't stop thinking about Wilbur and answers that Wilbur is the capital city of Pennsylvania.)

Author and You.   The answer is not in the text. This type of QAR asks for inferential or evaluative skills. The reader needs to think about what he or she already knows, think about what the author wrote, and put it together to answer the question. Example: "Fern will have to feed and care for Wilbur, feeding him with a baby bottle. She is 8 years old. If you have taken care of a pet, you know what a large responsibility that is. What will Fern have to do to keep Wilbur safe and well? Do you think she can do it?" (Answers to this type of question will vary.)

On My Own.   The answer to this type of question is not in the story. You can answer the question without reading the story. These can be either inferential or evaluative questions. Evaluative questions ask students to detect bias or to distinguish fact from opinion. Example: "Fern says that it is 'unfair' to kill Wilbur just because he is small and weak and is the runt of the litter. Is she right? Would it have been unfair? Suppose Fern slept late, and Wilbur was killed. Would you think Mr. Arable had done a terrible thing?" (Again, answers will vary.)

Teachers can assess levels of comprehension by developing a simple comprehension test using QARs. Select a story from a basal reader and write three questions of each type. Have the students read the selection silently and answer the questions. You should have a much clearer idea of each student's ability to answer literal, inferential, and evaluative questions.

Using Retellings to Assess the Literal Comprehension of Young Readers

The use of retellings has become a popular way of assessing the literal comprehension of young readers. Because many kindergarteners and first graders have limited ability to write, comprehension skills must be assessed orally. A retelling is less threatening than having the teacher fire questions at a 5-year-old, a procedure that all too often resembles an interrogation rather than an appropriate primary-grade assessment. After a student has read a story, the teacher asks the child to retell it.

There are two types of retellings. In an *unaided retelling*, the child simply is asked to retell the story (unaided retelling is also called *free retelling* or *recall*). The teacher provides no guidance. After the unaided retelling, the teacher usually proceeds with *aided recall* by asking the student if he or she remembers anything about a major component of the story the child failed to mention (aided recall is also called *probed recall*). For example, in a retelling of "Jack and the Beanstalk," if the child talked only about the ending of the story, the teacher might ask, "What happened before Jack climbed up the beanstalk?"

The teacher needs a checklist of items that a student should mention. The checklist can be organized by the literary elements (setting, characters, plot events). The teacher checks off each item if the child mentions it. Another way to organize the checklist is by the main events of the story, with supporting details listed under each main event. Again, it is important to note that retellings test literal comprehension. Unless they have been prompted by a question, children rarely make inferences or evaluate what they have read.

How to Assess Reading Comprehension Strategies

Effective teachers of reading model and teach strategies readers use to clarify the text's meaning (e.g., self-monitoring, re-reading, and summarizing). Unfortunately, it is difficult to assess these meta-cognitive comprehension strategies because all are internal, mental operations.

Oral Think-Alouds

Think-alouds can be used as a tool to assess which students monitor their reading, re-read what they don't understand, and are able to summarize what they have read. Any selection from a basal reader or a social studies or science textbook can be used as long as it will be challenging for the child who is reading it.

Think-alouds should be done individually; the teacher works with one student. The teacher asks the student to stop at two points in time: (1) any time he or she is having difficulty understanding the text; and (2) at the end of a paragraph or a page. Each time the child stops, the teacher says, "Please tell me anything that you are thinking about now."

Again, the reading selection should cause some difficulty. The teacher is looking for the following:

Does the child self-monitor? That is, does the student note when he or she is having difficulty (by saying such things as "This is hard" or "I don't get what's going on")? Does the student note when she or he is not having difficulty ("This is easy") or make a reasonable inference or speculation?

When in trouble, does the child select a repair strategy, such as re-reading? The child would say something like, "I better go back and read this paragraph again."

Does the child generate questions that the text will likely answer? The child might say, "I don't think Mr. Arable will kill the pig" or "I wonder how Fern will stop her father if he decides to kill Wilbur."

Does the child accurately summarize what he or she has read? The child would say something like, "Well, in that chapter, we learned how Fern saved Wilbur and he became her pet."

Written Assessments of Reading Comprehension Strategies

Note-taking, outlining, mapping, and logs all can be used to assess reading comprehension strategies. For assessment, the teacher would ask students to read something and, while reading, either take notes, make an outline, draw a story map, or keep a log.

The log can become the written version of the oral think-aloud process described in the previous section. Again, students are told to stop reading whenever they have difficulty and at certain predetermined points in the selection (end of a paragraph, end of a page). The student would write his or her thoughts in the log. One alternative is to ask the students to write questions they think will be answered by the rest of the selection. Proficient readers will write questions that flow logically from what has been read. Less able readers tend to write questions that have already been answered in the text.

HOW TO TEACH READING COMPREHENSION

Research shows that comprehension skills and strategies can be taught. Unfortunately, most elementary teachers attempt to teach comprehension through a single activity. A small group of children reads a story in a basal reader either silently or orally. Typically, one child reads aloud at a time. Every once in a while, usually at the end of a page, the teacher asks questions provided in the teachers' edition. This process tests comprehension to some degree by revealing which children understand the story, but unless the teacher does more than the ask-read-ask process, this process does little to teach comprehension and make children better readers.

Many types of activities can improve reading comprehension. For example, it is essential that teachers teach the meanings of key words that appear in a reading selection (covered in Chapter 9, "Vocabulary"). Also, good teachers help children become proficient readers of content-area texts (covered in Chapter 10, "Content-Area Literacy"). In this chapter, our focus will be on (1) the appropriate instructional context of comprehension lessons, (2) instruction before children read a text, (3) comprehension strategy instruction through reciprocal teaching, (4) comprehension skills instruction through question classification and answer verification using QARs, and (5) comprehension lessons using story structure.

The Context of Comprehension Lessons

There are many instructional models for teaching comprehension skills and strategies. "Guided Reading," an instructional format developed in New Zealand, is popular, although it is difficult to describe because there are many variations of this format. Major basal reading series, Open Court and Houghton Mifflin, both have specific formats for directed reading lessons. Whatever they are called, lessons focusing on reading comprehension should be taught according to the following principles:

- Comprehension lessons should be planned and implemented for a small group of children. Effective lessons require discussions, and for all children to be engaged, you need a small group.
- The children in the group should have the same instructional reading level. It is impossible to design comprehension lessons for students with widely different

reading levels. Both the material being read and the tasks the teacher poses must be aligned to the students' reading level.

- The material the students read should be at their instructional reading level to ensure that they do not struggle with word identification and they are challenged by the selection's content.
- As the year progresses, children in a class will be grouped and regrouped depending on their path of development. Children who are having an especially difficult time need individual attention.

Before Children Read

Before children read, teachers should (1) help children activate their background knowledge of the topic they are reading about and (2) teach the meanings of difficult words in the selection (see Chapter 9).

Direct Instruction to Activate Background Knowledge: KWL and PreP. Children will have a better chance of understanding what they are about to read if their teacher helps them call to mind what they know about the topic of the selection. In simple words, we don't know all that we know. This is called "activating background knowledge."

The use of KWL charts is a popular way for helping children activate their background knowledge. These charts help students activate, think about, and organize their prior knowledge. The teacher prepares a chart with three columns, *K, W,* and *L.* Let's assume a small group of children are about to read a story about penguins. The teacher asks the children, "What do you know about penguins?" and records their responses under the *K.* Then the teacher asks, "What would you like to learn about penguins?" and records the students' responses under the *W.* After the story has been read, the final column, under the *L,* is completed as the teacher asks, "What have we learned about penguins?"

PreP, the Pre-Reading Plan, is another way teachers can help their students call to mind what they know about a topic. PreP is a structured discussion with three steps:

1. Associations. The teacher says, "Tell me anything you think of when you hear the word *penguins.*" The teacher records these initial associations.
2. Reflections on the associations. The teacher asks some of the students who responded, "What made you think of (whatever the child said about penguins)?" Often, many new associations come forth during this part of the discussion.
3. Organizing associations. The teacher then asks, "Do any of you have new or different ideas or thoughts about penguins?" Many children will, at this point, recall additional information about the topic.

Strategy Instruction: Using Reciprocal Teaching

Reading strategies, once again, include self-monitoring, repair strategies (clarifying and re-reading), predicting, confirming, generating questions, and summarizing. Reciprocal teaching is an instructional process for teaching strategies. Research has shown that teachers who consistently use reciprocal teaching will help their students develop better reading comprehension.

Reciprocal teaching was developed to teach four strategies: generating questions, summarizing, clarifying (word meanings and confusing text), and predicting what might appear in the next paragraph. The teacher decides which strategy will be the focus of the lesson. Everyone has a copy of the same text, and these lessons usually focus on a short selection—a brief story or a chapter from a social studies or science textbook. In the initial lessons, the selection usually is read paragraph by paragraph; subsequent lessons ask the children to work with longer blocks of text.

The reciprocal teaching process follows the "gradual release of responsibility" model of instruction. The teacher initially models the strategy and then, over time, does less and less as the students do more and more. Over the course of a few weeks, the process would evolve as follows:

1. The teacher describes and defines the strategy and explains how and when to use it.
2. The teacher models the strategy using oral think-alouds to reveal the cognitive processes. For example, pretending to be confused, the teacher may say, "I am not sure why Sally wants to sell her computer. I am going to re-read the last two paragraphs" or "I don't know what a wardrobe is. I'd better look it up in the dictionary."
3. After lessons in which the teacher has described, defined, and modeled the strategy, the teacher and the small group of students collaboratively practice the strategy. If the group is working on generating questions, for example, the teacher and students would read a selection together. The teacher would stop at one point and say, "Let's see if we can write some questions that will be answered in the rest of this chapter." The teacher would come up with the first two questions; the students in the group would generate three more.
4. After collaborative lessons, the students are challenged to perform the strategy on their own in a "guided practice" format. The teacher "coaches" the students with corrective feedback as they use the strategy.
5. Finally, the students will be asked to use the strategy independently, with the teacher providing feedback only on the finished product.

Skills Instruction Through Question Classification and Answer Verification: Using QARs

A good way to help children acquire literal, inferential, and evaluative comprehension skills is to ask them to first classify the question and then verify their answer. Students having difficulty in reading typically have poorly developed inferential and evaluative comprehension skills. Usually they cannot answer inferential and evaluative comprehension questions because they treat every question as if it were literal, with an answer clearly stated in the text. One key to mastering inferential and evaluative questions is distinguishing different types of comprehension questions. Otherwise, children will waste a great deal of time trying to find the answers to inferential and evaluative questions when, in fact, the answers are not stated clearly in the text.

In the process of question classification and answer verification, children are challenged to first determine which type of question is being asked. Is it a literal question? Inferential? Evaluative? This will help them determine where the answer lies: "in the book" or "in their head." Once an answer is offered, students should then be challenged to verify their answer and explain how they "came up" with their answer.

The QAR system is good because it avoids the words *literal*, *inferential*, and *evaluative* and replaces them with a kid-friendly system. The four types of QARs, described previously in this chapter, are:

Right There. The answer to the question is in the text in a single identifiable sentence. These are literal questions.

Think and Search. The answer is in the text, but it is in two different parts of the text (the complete answer is not in a single sentence). This is a different type of literal question.

Author and You. The answer is not in the text. You need to think about what you already know and what the author said and put it together. These may be inferential or evaluative questions.

On My Own. The answer is not in the story. You can answer the question without reading the story. These may be inferential or evaluative questions.

The ultimate goal of QAR lessons is to prompt children to look at a question and say, "That is an 'author and you' question. I don't need to look for an answer in the text; I just need to think and write." Lessons focus on helping children identify and classify questions. A group of children reads a story in the basal reader. The teacher and the students look at a set of questions, such as those provided in the teachers' edition, and classify each question before trying to answer it.

At first, teachers may want to work on just distinguishing "right there" from "think and search" questions because both do have answer sources in the text. Next, the teacher could help children distinguish the two types of questions that do not have answers in the text: "author and you" and "on my own" questions.

Finally, after students have classified the question and provided an answer, they need to explain the basis of their answer. This is "answer verification." For "right there" and "think and search" questions, students will be able to cite a specific paragraph on a specific page. For "author and you" and "on my own" questions, the explanations will be more challenging because there will be several correct answers. Students must be able to provide some textual basis for their speculations or judgments (e.g., an incident in the story, a character's comment).

Story Structure: Using Story Maps, Story Grammars, and Story Frames

When students develop a sense of how stories are formed, they will be able to store information more efficiently, better remember details from all parts of a story, and recall story details with greater accuracy. Students can be taught to attend to story structure through story maps, story grammars, and story frames. These methods are an excellent way to improve literal comprehension.

For story maps, story grammars, and story frames, teachers first provide complete models to use to discuss the story. Then, the teacher provides "skeletal" maps, grammars, and frames. Students complete these while and after they read, with help from the teacher. Next, students are challenged to complete the skeletal maps, grammars, and frames on their own. Finally, older students should be able to create their own maps, grammars, and frames.

Story Mapping.   Story maps represent stories in a visual diagram by highlighting certain elements of the story. Making a story map helps students think about the structure of a story and how things relate to each other.

In some story maps, the story's title is placed in a circle in the center of the diagram and characters, events, and locations are placed in satellite positions around it. Lines show relationships. Other story maps actually look like things (fish, spiderwebs, etc.). The goal is to organize story information in graphic shapes like fish and fishbones (cause-and-effect relationships) or spiderwebs (details organized under identified subtopics, branched away from the web's center).

The simplest story map would look like this:

{Title of Story}

Beginning　　　　　　　　　　*Middle*　　　　　　　　　　*End*

Children would list story events under the appropriate section.

Story Grammars.   A story grammar is an outline. A common template for a story grammar would look like this:

Setting:

Problem:

   Event 1:
   Event 2:
   Event 3:

Resolution:

Story Frames.   Story frames are the simplest story structure device to complete; students just fill in the blanks. For example:

{Title of Story}

In this story, the problem starts when _____
After that _____

Next, _____
Then, _____

The problem is finally solved when _____
The story ends when _____

INTRODUCTION

A vocabulary is a set of words. It is important to note that each person has five different vocabularies.

Listening Vocabulary.   Your listening vocabulary consists of the words that you understand when listening to other people speak.

Speaking Vocabulary.   Your speaking vocabulary consists of the words you use when you talk. It is always smaller than your listening vocabulary.

Writing Vocabulary.   Your writing vocabulary consists of the words you use when you write.

Sight (Reading) Vocabulary.   Your sight vocabulary consists of the words you can recognize and correctly pronounce. We discussed this in Chapter 5, "Phonics and Other Word Identification Strategies."

Meaning (Reading) Vocabulary.   Your meaning vocabulary consists of the words you can understand when reading silently. The focus of this chapter is on helping children expand their knowledge of word meanings.

Research shows that teachers should plan four categories of activities to expand their students' meaning vocabularies:

1. Increase the amount of time children read independently and increase the different types of books they read.
2. Teach children the meanings of important words.
3. Teach children strategies for contextual and morphemic analysis so they can figure out the meanings of words they do not know.
4. Encourage word-consciousness.

HOW TO ASSESS VOCABULARY DEVELOPMENT

Assessing Word Meaning

For meaning vocabulary, teachers can select standardized, commercially published tests, like the California Achievement Tests (CAT) and the Stanford Achievement Tests (SAT); vocabulary tests that come with a basal reader series; or tests they have designed themselves to assess a student's level of word meaning. Here are some formats for assessing meaning vocabulary:

Use a Word in Sentence/Multiple Answer Options Format.   This is the most valid format for assessments of knowledge of word meaning. Standardized tests and the tests that come with a basal reader series usually adopt this format for testing meaning vocabulary. The key is that the target word, underlined or italicized, appears in a phrase or a sentence. It does not appear in isolation. Likewise, the possible definitions should all be phrases, not single words.

Choose a Synonym.   Another way to test knowledge of word meanings is to ask students to identify a synonym of a target word.

Analogies.   A third format that can be used to assess meaning vocabulary is analogies. Two words that have a relationship are listed together, and then the target word appears. The student must select a word that has that same relationship to the target word. For example, *head* is to *body* as _____ is to *mountain* (the correct answer is *peak*).

Match Definition to Word.   Finally, another possible way to assess word meaning is to provide children with a list of words and a list of possible definitions. Then they must match the proper definition with each word.

Tests of Morphemic Analysis

Tests of morphemic analysis assess student knowledge of prefixes, suffixes, root words, and compound words. These are sometimes called tests of "structural analysis." Some tests ask students to identify nonsense words with common prefixes or suffixes (i.e., *monotell*, *semidid*), but these are really tests of prefix and suffix identification, rather than meaning. Other, more meaning-oriented tests ask students to define common prefixes and suffixes (e.g., "What is the difference between a *test* and a *pretest*?").

HOW TO TEACH VOCABULARY

Once again, teachers should plan four categories of activities to expand the meaning vocabularies of their students: (1) increase the amount of time children read independently and increase the different types of books they read; (2) teach children the meanings of important words; (3) teach children strategies for contextual and morphemic analysis so they can figure out the meanings of words they do not know; and (4) encourage word-consciousness. The final section of this chapter will look at how teachers can help their students use dictionaries.

Independent Reading: Read More and Read More Types of Books

Research shows that children learn the meanings of thousands of words simply through independent reading. Many proficient readers have acquired large vocabularies by reading extensively. A phenomenon one authority called the "Matthew Effect" definitely takes place—more able readers tend to read more, and when they do, the gap between them and their less able classmates widens. (The descriptor comes from the Bible passage in the Book of Matthew about the rich getting richer.) Students who need to become better readers must enhance their meaning vocabularies. One way to achieve this goal is to help the child spend more time reading. Another is to expand the types of books the child reads. The more a child reads, the more words she or he will encounter in print. Although researchers cannot explain it, the more often a reader comes across a word, the better the chance the reader will acquire an understanding of the word's meaning. Reading books by different authors or in different genres exposes the reader to new types of words.

We will discuss how to increase student independent reading in Chapter 12, "Student Independent Reading."

Teaching the Meaning of Specific Words

Teachers should teach students the meanings of some words that will appear in selections they will read. There are dozens of effective techniques for teaching children the meaning of words. First, a couple of important points. Most teachers try to teach the meaning of too many words each week. Researchers at the University of Pittsburgh have shown there is a magic number: The "average" elementary school student can learn the meanings of about 350 to 400 words a year—about nine a week. Thus, teachers should carefully select the words they teach. The words selected should be ones that students don't know, that they are capable of learning, and that are important in that their meaning is essential if children are to understand the stories or textbook chapters they will read.

Although many alternatives exist, most teachers rely on two relatively ineffective techniques to teach the meanings of words. The teacher simply displays the word on the blackboard and then tells the children what it means. Likewise, asking children to look up the meaning of a word in a dictionary, without some discussion of the results, is also an ineffective way to teach meaning vocabulary. Here are some worthwhile alternatives:

Cluing Technique. Joan Gipe created the cluing technique as a way to teach the meaning of new words. The teacher creates four sentences for each word that will be taught. The first sentence uses the target word appropriately in a sentence. The second sentence describes the characteristics of the target word. The third sentence defines the target word in language the children will understand. The fourth sentence asks a question with the target word.

The students read the sentences or the teacher reads the sentences to them. Then the students write an answer to the question in the fourth sentence. Afterwards, the teacher and the students discuss their responses, focusing on the definition of the word. Here is an example for the word *unicycle*:

> *Fred's older brother rides around on a unicycle. This looks strange because a unicycle has only one wheel. A unicycle is like a bicycle, except it has only one wheel. Would you like to learn how to ride a unicycle?*

Contextual Redefinition. Contextual redefinition makes use of the context surrounding the target word and the power of cooperative learning. It is especially effective when teaching words from a story in a basal reader or from a chapter in a social studies or science textbook. First, the teacher finds the paragraph where the target word first appears in the basal reader (or textbook). For simple words, the teacher needs only to copy the sentence in which the target word first appears. For more difficult words, the teacher should copy the sentence preceding that sentence and the sentence superseding it (three sentences in all). The sentences can be placed on a worksheet or on the overhead projector. For example, for the target word *vigilantes*:

> *There was no system of government as we know it in the mining camps. The miners became vigilantes and caught and punished people whom they thought had*

committed crimes. People were sometimes caught by the vigilantes, given a quick trial, and hung all in the same day.

Contextual redefinition works best with a small group of children. The lesson proceeds as follows: First, the teacher displays the word and students guess what it means. Those who venture a guess should explain the rationale for their definition. Working as a group, the students come up with one "best-guess" definition. Then the students (or the teacher) read the three sentences. Now, the students guess again what the word means, using the sentences as a basis. Again, the group needs to reach a consensus. If at this point the students have not arrived at a reasonable definition, the teacher should display a dictionary definition.

Semantic Mapping (Also Called a Word Map or Semantic Webbing). Semantic maps are diagrams. They are particularly useful in pre-reading instruction because they not only teach the meanings of words, they also help children activate their prior knowledge of key concepts associated with the target word.

The teacher places the target word in the center of a circle. The circle can be written on the blackboard or on chart paper. The goal is to draw a web of words and phrases around the centered target word. The teacher may supply some words on the chart, but most should come from the students. As new words are suggested, their association to the target word is discussed. Closely related words should be circled and lines between groups of words should be drawn (these lines look like "rays" coming from the centered circle with the target word). For example, for the target word *dolphin*, one "satellite" group of words would relate to mammals (*breathes, doesn't lay eggs*), another to the physical characteristics of dolphins (*looks like a big fish, "smiles" at you*), and a third to other associations (*smart, talk to each other, named Flipper*).

Word Sort (Also Called List-Group-Label). In this vocabulary teaching activity, students sort a collection of words. A word sort works only if the target words can be placed in three, four, or five groups. The words should be placed on 3×5-inch cards. The teacher and the students discuss each word and then create categories. For example, for words from a story in a basal reader, the categories might be *characters, setting, events*. These categories are written on the board, and the students place each word in the correct category. This activity works well as a review of words previously learned.

Semantic Feature Analysis. Semantic feature analysis is a good teaching activity for a set of words that share at least one characteristic. It works well with words from social studies and science units. The teacher creates a grid or matrix that identifies traits of the target words. Along the vertical axis, the target words are listed. Along the horizontal axis, the traits are listed. Next to each word, the children place a + under each trait the word shares. Here is a semantic feature analysis for the teaching techniques just presented:

	Teaches Meaning	*Uses Context*	*Uses a Chart*
Cluing Technique	+	+	−
Contextual Redefinition	+	+	−
Semantic Map	+	−	+
Word Sort	+	−	+
Semantic Feature Analysis	+	−	+

Teaching Word Learning Strategies: Contextual Analysis

In addition to teaching the meanings of words, teachers should provide children with tools to figure out the meaning of unknown words when they read independently. Two strategies are particularly useful: contextual analysis and morphemic analysis.

Teaching Students to Identify Five Types of Contextual Clues. Many times, readers will be able to correctly guess the meaning of an unknown word by thinking about the words, phrases, and sentences surrounding that word. One technique for helping students use context is to teach them to identify five types of contextual clues:

1. *Definition contextual clues*: The author actually provides a definition for the target word in the text. This is very common in elementary social studies and science textbooks.
2. *Synonym contextual clues*: Another word in the paragraph is a synonym for the target word.
3. *Antonym contextual clues*: Another word in the paragraph is an antonym for the target word.
4. *Example contextual clues*: The author of the text has provided a definition of the target word by listing examples of the word in the text.
5. *General contextual clues*: There are words in the paragraph, often spread across several sentences, that will help the reader figure out the unknown word.

Teachers provide examples of each type of clue and model how they can be used. The teacher typically uses "think-alouds" to demonstrate how to use each type of clue. Gradually, the teacher releases responsibility by stating that the children must find a particular type of clue in the paragraph (e.g., "There is an antonym clue in this paragraph that will help you figure out the meaning of the word *clergy*").

Opin. An Opin sentence is a form of CLOZE, with only one word missing. For example:

During recess, Fred tripped on the _____ and skinned his knee (elephant, rug, asphalt).

One of the word options should clearly be wrong (in this case, *elephant*). A second choice should be close to being correct (*rug*). One of the three choices, of course, should be most correct (*asphalt*). Students work in groups of three to decide which word to place in the blank. First, each child makes a selection, then the group talks about their choices. The teacher works with children so that they use the other words in the sentence as clues for determining the correct choice.

Teaching Word Learning Strategies: Morphemic Analysis

Morphemic analysis requires students to look at the parts of words to determine their meaning. This is also called *structural analysis*. First, you should know some linguistic words and phrases relating to the structure of words.

Definitions. A *morpheme* is the most elemental unit of meaning in a language. In English, there are only two types of morphemes: some words and all affixes (prefixes and suffixes). Remember, not all syllables are morphemes, and some words have more than one morpheme.

Affixes are either *prefixes*, morphemes that appear before a root word, or *suffixes*, morphemes that appear at the end of a root word. Examples of prefixes are *non-*, *un-*, and *pre-*. Examples of suffixes are *-ment*, *-er*, and *-ly*.

Bound morphemes are prefixes and suffixes that cannot occur alone; they must be attached to a root word (*un-*, *-est*). A *free morpheme* can be uttered alone with meaning (for example, *test*).

Teachers should teach their students the following to help them unlock the definitions of unknown words: prefixes, suffixes, common root words, synonyms and antonyms, and Greek and Latin roots and affixes (such as *graph, morph, form*).

A Format for Teaching Prefixes, Suffixes, and Root Words.   As with phonics, you can either follow a whole-to-part or part-to-whole approach to teach students about root words and the use of prefixes and suffixes. In a whole-to-part lesson you would follow these steps:

1. Display several sentences, each with a word that contains the target prefix, suffix, or root word. For example, for the prefix *un-*:

   Roberto was <u>unafraid</u> when he entered the haunted house.
   The zookeeper <u>uncaged</u> the tiger when it was time to move him to another zoo.
   Thuy checked very carefully, but the letter was <u>undated</u>.
   The movie was so long it seemed to be <u>unending</u>.
   Leticia tried her best but she could not <u>untangle</u> the cord to the Christmas lights.

2. Read again the underlined target words and identify the key common element. You might want to circle the common prefix, suffix, or root word.
3. Work with the students to arrive at the meaning of the prefix, suffix, or root word. If they can't figure it out, tell them what it means.
4. Provide some other words with the common element, or see if the children can provide the words.

You may want to create a word wall of words that share the common element.
In a part-to-whole approach, you would use this sequence:

1. Display the prefix, suffix, or root word on the blackboard, in this case, *un-*. Tell the children what it means (in this case, *not* or *the opposite of*).
2. Prepare some 4 × 6-inch cards with root words that can be added to the prefix or suffix to make words. For root words, you will need to prepare cards with prefixes and suffixes on them. For example, for teaching *un-*, you would need cards that read *afraid, caged, ending, tangled*. For teaching the root word *cycle*, you would need cards that read *bi, tri, motor*. Add the cards to the element on the board and make new words.
3. Finally, help the children put each newly formed word into sentences, which can be written on the blackboard or on a piece of chart paper.

Encouraging Word-Consciousness

Finally, teachers can help students build their vocabularies by planning activities that develop word-consciousness. *Word-consciousness* is an interest in words and their meanings. Please note here that we are interested in playing with words, but not in the same way we discussed in Chapter 4, "Phonemic Awareness." There, the focus was on the sounds of words. Here, we are interested in the meanings of words.

Synonyms and Antonyms. A good way to expand the meaning vocabularies of children is to teach lessons and play games with synonyms (two words with similar meanings) and antonyms (two words with opposite meanings).

One way to teach synonyms is to choose five words, each with a clear synonym, and write a paragraph that contains each of them. Highlight the five words. The paragraph will give children contextual clues to figure out the meanings of the five words if they don't know them. Then provide children with a "bank" of 10 words—five of which are synonyms for the five target words, and the other five which are not synonyms for any of the five target words. Challenge children to come up with synonyms for the highlighted words. You can use the same process to teach antonyms by having the word bank include antonyms for the target words.

Once they have been introduced to word pairs that are either synonyms or antonyms, children can play many games. In one, the teacher divides the class in half. She gives a word, written on a card, to each child. For each word, some child has a word that is a synonym (or an antonym, if that is what the teacher is teaching). The children must then find their partners who have the synonym for their words.

Word of the Day. Some teachers foster word-consciousness by having a "word of the day." Sometimes the teacher selects the word, and sometimes the word comes from a child's question or comment. The word is displayed in large letters. The teacher should also present the word in context, in a paragraph, by using an overhead projector or a computer-based projection system. The teacher and the class should talk about the meaning of the word. If the word has a common prefix, suffix, or root, then other related words can be recorded. The teacher should stress the importance of the word and provide a rationale for the word's selection.

Playing with Words: Idioms and Puns. Idioms are phrases with the following characteristic: It is impossible to determine the phrase's meaning even if the meaning of each individual word is known. Examples are *It's raining cats and dogs* or *Don't look a gift horse in the mouth.* Puns involve the humorous use of a word, typically by playing with a word that has more than one meaning or substituting one word that sounds like another (e.g., one of Shakespeare's characters remarks about a person who has died, "*Yes, he is a grave man*"). Children like to build collections of idioms and puns and enjoy illustrating them.

Using the Dictionary

Finally, children can learn the meanings of words by looking for a definition in a dictionary. There are a number of cautions to note here. First, be sure that children use a developmentally appropriate dictionary, one with appropriate words, a large type-face, child-friendly definitions, and plenty of illustrations. Second, there are problems with relying on the dictionary to find the meaning of a word. If you are reading and stop to consult a dictionary, the slow process distracts you from the meaning of whatever you are reading. When the children find the target word, they may not be able to understand the definition they read. If the word has more than one definition, the child may not know which definition is appropriate for the word, given the context of the passage. Before children use the dictionary, they need these skills: how to alphabetize words; how to find and use guide words; and how to identify the applicable meaning for a word with multiple meanings. Teachers should prepare lessons that focus on the following:

- Understanding alphabetical order to the third, fourth, or fifth letter. You can't locate words in the dictionary unless you know how to alphabetize words.
- Using the guide words (first and last entry) that appear on each page of a dictionary. Efficient use of guide words will greatly facilitate the use of the dictionary.
- Dealing with multiple meanings. As an exercise, children should be given several words with multiple meanings (i.e., *foul*). Then they should be given sentences with different meanings of the word. For example: *Tucker hit a foul ball. There was a foul smell coming from the refrigerator.* Children should then match the appropriate dictionary meaning to each sentence.

Remember, it is important for teachers to first model the use of the dictionary, then provide students with a reasonable amount of guided practice using the dictionary, and then challenge them to find meanings of words in the dictionary independently.

INTRODUCTION

Content-area literacy refers to the reading and writing tasks that students complete while learning content. The content areas of the K–12 curricula include social studies, science, mathematics, health, and the study of the visual and performing arts (e.g., the history of painting, rather than how to paint). For the most part, however, content-area reading and writing focus on social studies and science. Students who are effective content-area readers also can read and understand information located in encyclopedias, in almanacs, and on Internet Web sites.

Elementary school children spend most of their time reading stories, which are examples of *narrative* text. Social studies and science textbooks, encyclopedias, and most Internet sites are examples of *expository* text. The purpose of an expository text is to inform the reader. Some elementary school children find reading expository texts to be a significant challenge.

Nonfiction books are another example of expository text. Today, most professionals in the field use the descriptor *information book*, rather than nonfiction, to label works that provide content knowledge.

Expository Text Structures

In Chapter 8, "Reading Comprehension," you read that many stories are written to follow a predictable pattern, and that teachers can use story grammars, story maps, and story frames to help children understand these patterns. Likewise, most social studies textbooks, science textbooks, and encyclopedia entries are written in standard patterns or structures. These expository text structures include:

Cause and Effect.   This structure is common in science textbooks, in which the author is showing that some phenomena result from some other phenomena. It also occurs in social studies textbooks when the author explains why a historical event occurred.

Problem and Solution.   In this type of expository text structure, the author presents a problem and then provides an explanation for the reader.

Comparison/Contrast.   In this structure, the writer examines the similarities and differences among two or more historical figures, events, or phenomena.

Sequence.   The author lists items or events in numerical or chronological order.

Description.   The author describes a topic by listing characteristics or features.

Teachers can use these text structures for three purposes: (1) to create a graphic organizer for students to examine before they read; (2) to create a study guide to help students understand the important points of a selection while and after they read; and (3) to assess the content-area reading comprehension of students.

Students can use expository text structures to become more efficient readers of content-area texts. Readers can use the author's organizational structure to make predictions about which information will be presented, to clarify information that seems contradictory, and to summarize the key points of a chapter.

Appendix G shows diagrams of these expository text structures.

HOW TO ASSESS CONTENT-AREA LITERACY

CLOZE

A CLOZE test can determine whether a student can comprehend a specific text. CLOZE can be used with short stories and novels. I mention it here because it is a tool for teachers who need to see whether a child can read a grade-level social studies or science textbook. It is difficult to use CLOZE with texts written below the second-grade level because their chapters do not contain enough words to create a CLOZE passage. A CLOZE test will tell you whether the text is at the child's independent, instructional, or frustration reading level.

CLOZE is short for "closure." Here is how it works: Let us say that a fourth-grade teacher wants to determine who among his students will have difficulty with the fourth-grade science textbook. The teacher would choose a chapter in the middle of the textbook and select a passage of at least 275 words, preferably at the beginning of a chapter. It is important that the children have not read the passage before the CLOZE test. Working on a word processor or with a photocopy of the pages in the passage, the teacher deletes every fifth word, starting with the second sentence. There should be 50 blanks. The passage should conclude with a complete sentence.

The teacher explains the CLOZE test format to the child: The child reads the passage once without doing anything. Then, he or she reads the passage and attempts to write in the missing words in the blanks created by the teacher. To score the CLOZE, the teacher calculates how many of the missing words the child was able to provide. Count as correct only exact replacements.

Authorities do not agree on the standards for determining independent, instructional, and frustration levels for CLOZE texts. The following, however, is fairly standard:

Independent Reading Level.   The student provided over 60% of the missing words. This is good! The student will be able to read the textbook with little assistance from the teacher.

Instructional Reading Level.   The student provided between 40% and 60% of the missing words. This is okay! The student will be able to read the text if the teacher plans effective content-area reading lessons, develops a pre-reading guide, or provides study guides to help the student understand the information presented.

Frustration Reading Level.   The student provided fewer than 40% of the missing words. This result must be taken seriously. It means the student will have difficulty with the textbook even if the teacher provides a great deal of assistance. Teachers will need to find other ways to help the child acquire the information the text presents (easier books, charts and diagrams, audiovisual resources, or peer tutors).

Using Text Structures

Teachers can use text structures to assess student comprehension of a content-area text. The teacher provides a "skeleton" and the students complete the missing parts. For example, take another look at Appendix G. The Venn diagram is a good way to show a comparison. A test for a science textbook chapter on the planet Mars might use a Venn diagram, with one circle for Earth and the other for Mars. Students would be challenged to list three things unique to Earth (*abundance of water*), three things the planets share (*polar caps*), and three things unique to Mars (*atmosphere almost entirely carbon dioxide*).

Multilevel Questions

In Chapter 8, I described how to use the QAR system to create simple tests of a child's mastery of comprehension skills, especially the "higher order" skills of inference and evaluation. Teachers should use the QAR hierarchy with social studies and science textbooks to assess their students' ability to answer all types of questions. Again, it is essential to see if students can answer the think-and-search, author-and-you, and on-my-own type of questions. Bloom's Taxonomy can also be used to design a simple test of all levels of reading comprehension.

Teacher Observation/Anecdotal Records

Teachers can gather useful data about the content-area reading performance of their students by simply observing their behavior and taking notes. For example, when students are asked to read in their science textbook and retrieve information by completing a chart, a teacher should note who completes the task easily and who struggles. Likewise, if a student trying to find information in an encyclopedia is unable to use guide words to locate the appropriate entry, the teacher should make a note of that. Over the course of time, these informal notes begin to add up and can be used to support your conclusions. If, for example, you think that Fred has difficulty reading his social studies textbook, then it helps if you have anecdotal notes from September 11, October 2, and October 16 verifying that conclusion.

Readability of Texts

One other evaluation concept needs to be explained here. *Readability* is a measure of the difficulty of a text. Several readability formulas exist that teachers can use to determine whether a child can read a specific book (assuming the child's independent reading level is known). Readability formulas are applied to a passage from a textbook or an information book. These formulas measure the semantic difficulty of a text by calculating word length and the number of syllables in the passage and the syntactic difficulty of the text by calculating the number of words in sentences. Two well-known readability formulas are the Fry Readability Graph and the Raygor Readability Estimate.

Your reading methods text will explain how to administer a readability formula. There have always been many questions about the validity of these formulas because they don't take into account the quality of the text's writing, nor do they measure a student's interest in the topic the text addresses. It is always easier to read something well written because information presented is more interesting. Finally, the utility of readability formulas is diminished by the time it takes the teacher to use them.

Once again, if a teacher has determined a child's independent, instructional, and frustration reading levels through an IRI, then a readability formula would tell the teacher how a textbook or an information book from the library "fits" a child's reading ability.

HOW TO TEACH CONTENT-AREA LITERACY

Our discussion of content-area literacy teaching will focus on instructional strategies and activities that help students (1) comprehend their social studies and science textbooks, (2) become more efficient in the specialized reading experiences of *skimming* and *scanning*, and (3) improve their study skills.

Improving Comprehension of Content-Area Textbooks

The instructional strategies covered in Chapter 8 are, for the most part, the same ones teachers should use when students read content-area texts. It is important that teachers use content-area textbooks to teach reading strategies with reciprocal teaching. Teachers should use content-area reading assignments to work on question classification and answer verification, too. Effective vocabulary teaching, so important when students are reading stories, is especially important with expository texts. Perhaps the best way to frame our discussion is to answer the question, "What comprehension-building instructional activities are unique to content-area reading?" We will examine (1) linking what has been learned previously to the present reading assignment; (2) previewing the content of the reading assignment with a graphic organizer; (3) focusing student attention on essential information with study guides, learning logs, and data retrieval charts; and (4) teaching students how to use text structures to better comprehend content-area textbooks.

Before Students Read: Linking to What Has Been Learned Previously. Before students read, teachers should help students activate their background knowledge of the topics covered in the text, build students' vocabularies by teaching them the definitions of unfamiliar words, link the content of the text to what children have learned previously, and preview the important information students will learn when they read. We covered two instructional strategies for activating background knowledge in Chapter 8: KWL and PreP. Either can be used with content-area texts. The effective teaching of vocabulary was covered in Chapter 9, "Vocabulary."

It is important that teachers help students find the connection between the content learned previously and the content of the day's reading assignment. This is not important with lessons based on stories in a basal reader because each story usually is unrelated to the stories before and after it. Chapters in a social studies or science textbook, however, usually are related to each other. In fact, in many instances students will be able to better understand the information presented in one chapter if they review what they have learned previously. For example, a chapter on the habitats of amphibians may be preceded by a chapter on the anatomy of amphibians. Unless students recall the unique aspects of amphibians' bodies, they won't understand why they live where they do.

There are many ways to link information students will be expected to learn to what they have learned previously:

- *Review of a KWL chart, a data retrieval chart, or a summary chart.* If the class completed a KWL chart on the material they learned previously, the chart could be re-examined. Data retrieval charts and summary charts will be described later in this chapter. They could be used to review the material students read the day before a content-area reading lesson.
- *Re-Read.* Another easy way to review information presented in a previous chapter of a social studies or science text is to take a second look at that chapter. In other words, before reading Chapter 4, the teacher will have the students open their textbooks to Chapter 3. Together, the class again will look at illustrations and discuss major chapter headings. Students might also be asked to re-read a summary of the chapter.

Before Students Read: Previewing with a Graphic Organizer. A graphic organizer, prepared by the teacher, is used before students read. It provides students with an overview of what they will read, usually for an entire chapter in a social studies or science textbook. A well-designed graphic organizer presents the key points of a chapter in an easy-to-read format. It is, in fact, a simple outline of the chapter (graphic organizers also are called *structured overviews*). Graphic organizers are based on the text structures included in Appendix G: cause and effect, problem and solution, comparison and contrast, sequence, and description. Remember, a graphic organizer is prepared by the teacher, provides an overview of what students will read, has relatively few words, and is examined before students read. Appendix H is an example of a graphic organizer.

Another way to preview what students will read is through a summary chart. A summary chart is a list of sentences, usually no more than five, stating the key points of a chapter. For example, a teacher prepared this chart to preview a chapter about the functions of California missions:

Summary Chart—What Happened at the Missions

The missions were:

- *Churches—To convert the natives to Christianity*
- *Forts—To defend Spain's claim to California*
- *Farms—To produce food for people at the mission*
- *Factories—To produce things needed at the mission*

While and After Students Read: Focusing Student Attention with Study Guides. When students are asked to read their social studies or science textbooks, teachers should emphasize essential information in the selection. This should be done while students read and immediately thereafter. There are a number of ways teachers can highlight the important information in a content-area reading assignment. Here, our focus is on study guides; in the next section we look at learning logs and data retrieval charts. Middle school and high school teachers have used study guides for years (also called *reading guides*). They can also be used effectively with elementary school children. The purpose of all study guides is to focus student attention on key information in the text. Children complete the guides while working in small groups, the guides may be completed by the whole class with the teacher's assistance, or children may be asked to complete them individually. Study guides can be constructed in a number of formats:

Study Guides Based on Text Structures. Study guides based on the text's structure are particularly effective because they direct students to use the text's structure to find the missing information (once again, the text structures are in Appendix G). This type of study guide resembles a graphic organizer, but it has either questions or "fill-in-the-blanks" in it. The students complete the guide while they are reading. A study guide based on the text structure of cause and effect is shown in Appendix I.

Key Questions Study Guide. The simplest study guide is a set of questions based on the most important information in the text. For children who have difficulty reading content-area material, some teachers include the page number(s) where the answers can be found. A simple study guide like this would be:

Study Guide—The Russians in California
Pages 122–123

1. Where in Alaska had the Russians built a trading post?
2. Why did Nikolai Rezanov sail to San Francisco?
3. How long did the Russians stay at Fort Ross? Why did they leave?

Three-Level Study Guide. This type of study guide, sometimes called an *interlocking guide*, typically defines three levels of comprehension: literal, interpretative, and applied. As originally conceived, the three-level guide consisted of statements written by the teacher; students then check those that are true. Other three-level guides consist of two or three questions from each of the levels of comprehension. Here we will base our guide on three levels of comprehension: literal, inferential, and evaluative. The sample three-level guide that follows uses that classification and features a combination of true/false statements and questions:

Three-Level Study Guide—The Articles of Confederation
Pages 77–80

Literal

Check each statement that is true:

_____ The Articles of Confederation were the first "constitution" of the United States.

_____ The Articles provided for a Senate and House of Representatives.

Inferential

Check each statement that is true:

_____ Ambitious politicians who wanted to be president would be frustrated if we still used the Articles.

_____ It would have been difficult for the United States to become a world power while under the Articles.

Evaluative

If you thought the Articles were a better set of rules than our current Constitution, what three arguments would you make?

Learning Logs.   Another way teachers can highlight important information is to ask students to keep learning logs while they read content-area material. A learning log is a type of journal students use to record many things: their questions, plans for projects, and ideas for further study. Teachers should use prompts or questions to focus students on essential information. Sometimes the prompts are general (e.g., *List three things you learned today about the Gold Rush in California*), or they may be focused (*Write a letter to your parents explaining why you want to go to California to hunt for gold*).

Data Retrieval Charts.   Data retrieval charts allow students to record information in a framework provided by the teacher. They do not require a great deal of writing, and they focus students on the essential information in a selection. Following is a data retrieval chart for a chapter on the United States Congress.

Data Retrieval Chart

The United States Congress

	House of Representatives	*Senate*
Number of legislators		
Term of office		
Minimum age		
Presiding officer		

Specialized Reading Experiences: Skimming, Scanning, In-Depth Reading

Children will have different purposes when reading content-area material, depending on what they hope to accomplish. The process of reading a story or a chapter from a social studies or science textbook is the same—you start at the beginning and read until you come to the end. Many times, however, students need to retrieve only a small piece of information. For example, a teacher asks students to find out the unusual coincidence of the deaths of John Adams and Thomas Jefferson. Students would not want to read the entire encyclopedia entry on either man. Instead they would scan the entry, read quickly, and skip about until they found the dates of each man's death. (The coincidence is that both Adams and Jefferson died on the same day—July 4, 1826—exactly 50 years after the signing of the Declaration of Independence.)

Skimming.   Skimming is an extraordinarily fast reading of a text, usually for purposes of preview or review. While skimming, the reader is looking for key words, subtitles, and important sentences. This type of reading develops only with practice. Teachers should model skimming and then challenge students to skim a page or two on their own. Then the teacher should highlight the key words, phrases, and sentences on those pages.

Scanning.   Scanning, on the other hand, is a rapid reading to find specific information. The reader must swiftly sweep over the page, looking for a path to the correct details. As with skimming, this type of reading is learned with practice. The teacher should model scanning and then provide guided practice for children.

In-Depth Reading.   Finally, some assignments require students to read a content-area selection very carefully, aiming for a full understanding of the information presented. There are many tools students could use to assist themselves with this type of reading. They could develop their own outline, make their own pattern guide, or record important information and their questions in a learning log.

SQ3R is an old technique, first proposed in 1946, for helping students become proficient at in-depth reading. SQ3R stands for *survey, question, read, recite, review.* First, students survey the chapter, looking at the title, subtitles, captions, and anything in bold type. Next, they write two or three questions they think the chapter will answer. Third, the students read the chapter, looking for answers to their questions. Fourth, students test themselves on the material presented in the chapter, stating aloud key points. Finally, students periodically review what they have learned, using their written questions and answers as a guide.

STUDY SKILLS

Study skills refer to locating and retrieving information from such reference materials as almanacs, atlases, encyclopedias, and now Internet Web sites. There are some things teachers should cover with their students.

Encyclopedias

Lessons on the Organization of an Encyclopedia. Teachers should help students understand that information is organized by topics, called *entries*, that are arranged in different volumes in alphabetical order. For example, a first lesson might involve showing students a full set of encyclopedias. Then, the teacher would present some sample entries (*archery, Wisconsin, insects*) and ask students to identify the volume where the entry would be located.

Lessons on How to Use the Index, Guide Words, and Cross-References. Once students understand the organization of an encyclopedia, the teacher should then teach how to swiftly find information by using the index, the guide words on each page, and the cross-references within each entry. The essential task here is to give children topics and then help them find the relevant pages as quickly as possible.

How to Scan for Specific Information. Finally, once students have located the relevant page number for an entry, they need to practice scanning to find the information they need.

Alternatives to Note-Taking

Most elementary school children find it very difficult to take notes while reading reference material. This is an important skill because it allows the reader to preserve important information he or she has found in an almanac, atlas, encyclopedia, or Web site. Here are two alternatives to standard note-taking for elementary children:

I-Charts. The use of I-Charts (information charts) will help children retrieve and preserve information from reference sources. The I-Chart is a sheet of paper containing the following information: the student's name, the student's research topic, a subtopic of that topic, a section entitled, "what I already know," a place to write new information, a place to write the bibliographic information about the reference source, a space for "other related information," a space for "important words," and a space for new questions. Each time a student consults a reference source, he or she completes an I-Chart.

Data Retrieval Charts. These were described previously. The teacher creates the framework for the chart and the students write information in the appropriate places.

CHAPTER 11

Literary Response and Analysis

INTRODUCTION

Many authorities in the field of reading instruction have called for a "balanced" approach to reading instruction. Experiences with literature provide children opportunities to use their acquired skills and strategies to read, discuss, write, and perform.

"Literary response and analysis" refers to a variety of experiences students have with literary works written for young readers. Children should have opportunities to *respond* to literature orally and in writing. Teachers should ask open-ended questions to allow their students to respond freely to the books they have read (e.g., "Tell me the first thing that comes to your mind when you think of *Out of the Dust*"). Teachers should also ask more direct questions to encourage response, such as, "Do you know any people who remind you of Billie Jo?"

Literary *analysis* focuses on the literary elements: character, setting, plot, theme, mood, style. Teachers should help students see how writers use such figurative language as similes and metaphors in novels and poetry. Our students should learn to recognize the features of different literary genres (e.g., mysteries and science fiction). Finally, students also should be asked how books reflect the perspectives of the time and place when they were written.

Teachers should have a well-planned literature program. Teachers are responsible for selecting high-quality literature for their students to read. Teachers should plan a variety of lessons that: (a) provide instruction in literary concepts, (b) offer opportunities to respond to literature, and (c) challenge students to analyze literary text structures and elements. Thus, we are talking about more than merely asking children to check out a book from the school or classroom library, read it, and then fill out some type of book report form.

HOW TO ASSESS LITERARY RESPONSE AND ANALYSIS

Types of Assessments

Students Read and Teacher Reads Aloud. Teachers should assess literary understanding by asking students to respond to and analyze both books that children have read themselves and books that the teacher reads aloud.

Oral and Written. Teachers evaluate students' response and analysis through oral and written assessments. For younger students especially, it is important that assessment be done orally. Many children cannot express in writing all their thoughts and feelings about books.

Free and Focused. It is important that the assessment of literary understanding be both free and focused. Free response requires the use of open-ended prompts such as, "Who has something they would like to say about *The Polar Express* by Chris Van Allsburg?" or "Write anything you want about *The Polar Express*."

Focused prompts tend to use the literary elements as a basis for questions. For example, "How are Alyce in *The Midwife's Apprentice* and Billie Jo in *Out of the Dust* alike? How are they different?" (Questions based on character.) "We have read two books by Margaret Wise Brown and two books by Dr. Seuss. Do these authors tell their stories the same way?" (Question based on style.)

Analysis of Results

As teachers analyze oral and written responses, they should see their students do each of the following:

Incorporate Literary Elements into Their Analysis of Books. Some examples: Do students focus on the characters in a story? Do they mention specific incidents that help the reader understand a character? Do children ever talk or write about the setting of the story? Do they notice how the story's time and place influence what is happening? Do students understand the plot device of conflict? Can they identify the point in a story when the plot's central conflict is resolved?

Make Connections to the Literature They Read. We want our students to see the relationship between the literature they read and each of the following:

- Other books, called *intertextual connections*. For example, can children talk or write about similar characters or settings in two different books?
- Their own lives, called *personal connections* or *text-to-self connections*. For example, when asked, can students link a book to their own lives by mentioning a personal challenge similar to one faced by a character in a book?
- The world around them, called *text-to-world connections*. For example, can children find a connection between an event in a book and a current event?

Provide Evidence from a Text to Support Their Responses. Finally, are children able to cite specific events or descriptions in a story to support the perspectives they have stated or written? For example, after a child reads *Holes* by Louis Sachar, she writes, "Stanley grew up during the story." Can this student cite an example of how Stanley changed during his experience at Camp Green Lake?

Participation Checklists

Finally, some teachers use checklists to evaluate students as they participate in literature-related activities. The results of such a checklist can be compared over the course of the school year. A checklist might include items such as:

- Promptly selects a new book after finishing another
- Maintains an accurate log of all books read
- Listens attentively during discussions of books
- Comments reflect a thorough understanding of the book

- Asks questions that challenge perspectives of other students
- Comments about each of the following during a discussion:

  Character
  Setting
  Plot
  Theme
  Style
  Mood

HOW TO TEACH LITERARY RESPONSE AND ANALYSIS

Responding to Literature

To provide the best possible instructional setting for children to respond to literature, teachers should:

Select Literature from a Wide Range of Eras, Perspectives, and Cultures. The first job of the teacher is to ensure that students are exposed to a variety of high-quality books. Some of these books will be read aloud by the teacher; others will be read by the children, either independently or in small groups. The best children's books provide excellent opportunities for children to respond to, and analyze, literature. Teachers should be aware of books that have won awards. All classrooms should have books that have won the two most prestigious awards: the Newbery and Caldecott Medals, which are each given annually by the American Library Association. The Newbery Medal is awarded to the best children's book written by an American author (usually a novel). The Caldecott Medal is given to the best-illustrated American picture book. Lists of these award-winning books and illustrators can be located in libraries, your college reading and children's literature textbooks, and online at www.ala.org.

Implement Instructional Formats That Encourage Response to Literature. There are a variety of instructional formats teachers can choose from to teach literature:

- In the *core book* approach, each member of a class has a copy of an important work in children's literature. All students read the book, or listen to their teacher read it, and complete a variety of assignments that encourage response and analysis.
- *Literature units* expose children to a variety of good books that share a common element, which may be the same author, theme, or genre. This format also is called *text sets*.
- During *literature study groups*, a small group of children all read, respond, and analyze the same book. These groups are also called *grand conversation groups* or *book clubs*.
- All classroom schedules should allow time when children can read books they have selected at their own pace. A common descriptor for this period of silent reading is Sustained Silent Reading (SSR). Some teachers expand this *self-selected, self-paced* component into a model called *Reader's Workshop*.

Require Students to Keep Literature Logs. Students should keep records of, and write about, the books they have read. Many teachers require students to keep a journal dedicated to their reading experiences with literature (these can be called *literature logs*, *literature journals*, or *reading logs*). Teachers should use a variety of prompts to stimulate written response. In addition to the open-ended and focused questions mentioned several times in this chapter, some teachers use "quotes and notes." Each child selects a sentence from a book he or she has read, copies it verbatim in his or her journal, and then writes a comment about the quote underneath it. In "double-entry journals," each child writes a comment about a book and then leaves space for the teacher or another student to write a reply.

Plan Discussions about Literature on a Regular Basis.   The role of the teacher varies during these discussions. Usually the goal of the teacher is to facilitate, not dominate any discussion. The more the teacher prompts individual children to respond to the literature, the better. When the teacher wants to focus oral response on a specific part of a book, such as a character, then he or she must ask more specific questions.

Analyzing Literature

Describing and Analyzing Story Elements.   Literary elements are at the center of instruction related to the analysis of literature. Teachers should directly teach each element. For example, older students should know the functions of setting in a story: to clarify conflict, serve as the antagonist, amplify character, establish mood, and serve as a symbol. The literary elements also should be the basis for many of the questions teachers ask children about the books they have read. Following is a brief summary of the literary elements:

Character.   In children's literature, characters usually are people. Some children's books have animals, plants, or inanimate things as characters (a stuffed animal, for example). Older students should be able to identify the protagonist(s) and antagonist(s) in a novel. The protagonist is the main character of the story, or in more literary terms, the character who "pushes toward" something. In colloquial terms the antagonist is the "bad guy," the character who pushes against the protagonist and tries to block him or her from achieving the goal.

Plot.   The sequence of events in a story is its plot. Many novels and plays written in English follow a plot structure that includes an introduction; rising action, during which the reader is introduced to conflict or complication; a climax when the conflict is resolved; and then falling action to wrap things up (called the *denouement*). Some stories break the normal flow of events with flashbacks and flash-forwards, which present events out of chronological order.

Setting.   Teachers should help students understand that the setting of a book is both the time and the place of the story. Settings in a story can be described as either *backdrop* or *integral* or somewhere in between. A story with a backdrop setting has a vaguely defined setting and could take place in a number of places or times (like most fairy tales). Integral settings are fully described and the story can only take place in that time and in that place (like most historical fiction).

Mood.   Mood is the feeling you have (spooky, comforting, majestic, etc.) when you are reading the story. In picture books, illustrations convey the mood. Scary moods usually are represented with dark colors and with things that are literally or figuratively cloaked or are only partially revealed. Joy and happiness typically are established with lots of light and bright colors. In novels, authors create mood by using descriptive words. A mood of suspense and impending danger can be created by foreshadowing (giving the reader a hint of the trouble ahead).

Theme. A story's theme, its important message, is usually a comment about the human condition. Theme can be clearly stated (explicit), or the reader must infer it (implicit). For example, the Newbery-winning book *Out of the Dust* has an explicit theme. Author Karen Hesse states, "You can stay in one place and still grow." On the other hand, readers must infer the theme of "the grass isn't always greener on the other side of the fence" in *The Little House* by Virginia Lee Burton. Even our youngest students can discern a book's central message if they are taught what to look for and how to look for it.

Style: Analyzing Figurative Language. Style is the way authors use words; it is the way illustrators use visual images. It is not the *what* of the story; it is *how* the story is told. Words have both a literal meaning and a figurative meaning. Figurative language is the use of words in a nonliteral way that gives them meaning beyond their everyday definition and provides an extra dimension to the word's meaning. Some examples of figurative language are:

- *Hyperbole.* An exaggerated comparison (example: "scared to death")
- *Metaphor.* An implied comparison (example: "The road was a river of moonlight")
- *Personification.* Giving human traits to nonhuman beings or inanimate objects. (example: "The crickets sang in the grasses. They sang the song of summer's ending.")
- *Simile.* One of the simplest figurative devices, a stated comparison between unlike things using the words *like* or *as* (example: "He was as big as a house")
- *Symbol.* A person, object, situation, or action that operates on two levels of meaning—the literal and the symbolic (example: in *The Polar Express*, the small bell is a symbol for the true meaning of Christmas).

Recognizing Features of Literary Genres. Genres are categories, or types, of stories. Teachers can teach children how to recognize the features of different literary genres. This can be done first by exposing children to several examples of a particular genre and then, through direct instruction, listing their common elements. The following genres cover most children's books:

Traditional Literature. These stories have their origins in oral storytelling and have survived through generations. Examples of folktales are cumulative tales (such as *The House That Jack Built*), pourquoi tales (which explain a natural phenomenon, such as *Why Mosquitos Buzz in People's Ears*, by Verna Aardema), trickster tales (B'rer Rabbit from Uncle Remus), and fairy tales (stories full of enchantment and magic). Traditional literature also includes tall tales (with much exaggeration), fables (which teach a lesson), and myths (which people created to explain the world around them).

Modern Fantasy. Modern fantasy includes those stories that are magical or play with the laws of nature and have known authors. This includes animal fantasy, with beasts that can talk; stories with toys and dolls that act like people; and stories with tiny humans.

High Fantasy. This is a popular type of modern fantasy for older children. High fantasy has a struggle between good and evil set in a fantastic world. The hero or heroine of the story usually goes on a quest of some sort. Examples include *The Lion, the Witch, and the Wardrobe*, by C. S. Lewis, and the Harry Potter books by J. K. Rowling.

Science Fiction.   This is a type of modern fantasy similar to high fantasy with one important difference: The story features some "improved" or "futuristic" technology. Science fiction is the genre of time machines, spaceships that travel at the speed of light, and holographic worlds.

Contemporary Realistic Fiction.   These stories take place in the present day in the real world. They can be humorous or quite serious. Examples include the Ramona Quimby books by Beverly Cleary and recent Newbery winners such as *Walk Two Moons* by Sharon Creech and *Missing May* by Cynthia Rylant.

Historical Fiction.   Historical fiction includes realistic stories that are set in the past. Good historical fiction makes the past come alive to young readers, as does *Roll of Thunder, Hear My Cry* by Mildred Taylor and *Island of the Blue Dolphins* by Scott O'Dell.

Biography.   Biographies are information books that tell the story of a real person's life. There are excellent picture book biographies written for young readers (popularized by the author Diane Stanley).

Informational Books.   Once called "nonfiction," informational books should present accurate information about something. These books, of course, are not stories. There are informational books written for children about virtually any topic you can imagine. Different from fiction, the style of informational books places special demands on the young reader (we discussed this in Chapter 10, "Content-Area Literacy").

Analyzing Ways in Which a Literary Work Reflects the Traditions and Perspectives of a Particular People or Time.   Literature can provide considerable insight about people who lived in the past and the many different cultural groups who live today. Literature has the potential to give us perspectives unlike our own. First, teachers must select books that accurately portray the way people may have viewed events of the past. In *Roll of Thunder, Hear My Cry*, Mildred Taylor provides young readers with an African American view of life in the segregated southern United States in the 1930s. Laura Ingalls grew up on the Great Plains in the late 19th century. Students can analyze her books to see how settlers dealt with the challenges of day-to-day living and see the harsh and stereotypical attitudes of European Americans towards Native Americans at that time. To provide balanced, multiple views of people other than European or American whites, teachers must share authentic books written by and for African American, Native American, Hispanic American, Asian American, and international authors and illustrators.

To accomplish this goal, teachers must make a character's perspective the focus of a lesson. This requires readers to look beyond the entertainment of the story to find specific passages that reveal the attitudes of different people in a certain time and place.

Student Independent Reading

INTRODUCTION

The instructional practices described in this chapter, like those covered in the previous chapter, provide opportunities for teachers to achieve a "balanced" reading program. Much of our discussion has been about how to directly teach reading skills and strategies, especially in the areas of phonemic awareness, phonics, spelling, comprehension, and vocabulary. Balance is achieved when these skills and strategies lessons are combined with opportunities for children to apply what they have learned, as they read a variety of good books and write about them.

Independent reading refers to reading at times other than as a part of a teacher-directed lesson. The material children read independently will usually be fiction, but should also include biographies, information books, magazines, and newspapers. Teachers should guide students to high-quality children's books and, in some cases, assign books for their students to read. Most independent reading, however, should be self-selected and self-paced. Reading is self-selected if the child chooses what she or he will read, and it is self-paced if the child reads the book with no externally imposed deadline.

Independent reading plays a critical role in a child's overall development, not just in the area of literacy. It is critical in other academic areas and in children's moral and ethical growth. Consider the following potential advantages of independent reading:

1. Provides greater familiarity with language patterns
2. Increases reading fluency
3. Increases vocabulary
4. Broadens knowledge in the content areas
5. Motivates further reading

HOW TO ASSESS STUDENT INDEPENDENT READING

Effective reading teachers are able to connect children with books that are just right for them. Because these books will be written at the child's independent reading level, they will be easy to read. They also will be written by favorite authors, in a favorite genre, or on a favorite topic. To find the right book for each child, teachers will need to know the child's independent reading level and reading interests. Teachers also should collect data on the books children read and on each child's independent classroom reading behavior.

Interest Inventory

Reading interest inventories are surveys of student reading behavior. They should be given orally to younger children; older students can write their answers on the inventory itself. These inventories include two types of questions: (1) those that try to determine to what extent the child values reading as a recreational activity; and (2) those that try to determine the child's reading preferences. Questions on an interest inventory might include:

- "If your teacher said you can spend one hour doing any school activity you wanted, what would you choose?"
- "How much time each day do you spend reading books at home?"
- "Who is your favorite author?"
- "Which of the following types of books do you like to read? Check as many as you like:

  Animal stories
  Fairy tales
  Mysteries
  Historical fiction (stories that take place in the past)
  Adventures
  High fantasy (such as the Harry Potter books)"

As with any form of survey, teachers should interpret the results of an interest inventory cautiously, especially with older students. Many students have learned that reading is important to teachers and thus will claim to read a lot more than they really do. The results of an interest inventory should be used in concert with the data gathered from student reading logs and your records of individual conferences.

Individual Conferences

Although they require one-on-one settings, teachers should hold regular, individual conferences with their students. During and immediately after these conferences, teachers should take notes. More recently some teachers have been recording these notes on laptop computers. Each child comes to the conference with his or her journal, where responses to the completed books have been written; his or her reading log (a record of the books read); and the book he or she is currently reading. The teacher uses the conference to discuss what the child has read, to help the child find new books to read, and to work on a skill or strategy the child has not mastered. The child may read to the teacher or the teacher may read to the child. The conferences can be expanded to include analysis and discussion of the child's writings.

Even if the conferences are held as infrequently as every two weeks, they yield important data. The teacher will learn about the student's reading interests and ability. The results of the conferences can be compared with the information gained through the interest inventory and the student's reading log.

Student Reading Logs/Journals

Each student should keep a record of the books he or she has read independently. A child in Grade 1 or 2 can write the name of each book, the book's author, the date he or she finished the book, and a personal response on an index card. The cards can be held together with yarn or stored in a file box. Older children should enter the same information on a reading log, which is kept in a folder. Yes, it is true that some children may commit fraud and enter books they haven't finished to impress the teacher. The results of individual conferences and common sense, however, will allow you to determine who has been "fudging." These reading logs reveal important information about the independent reading habits of your students.

In the previous chapter, I wrote that teachers should require students to write journal responses to the books they have read. Although the substance of those responses is useful primarily to determine students' development in the areas of response and analysis, the responses can also be used to make judgments about students' level of independent reading. Simply put, children who read a lot independently will have full responses to more books than children who do not.

Data on Reading Behavior at School and at Home.   It is a good idea to write anecdotal notes about the reading behavior of your students at school. For example, at lunch on a rainy day, who decides to read? During your visits to the school library, who thoughtfully selects a book and begins reading and who, on the other hand, seems to waste time and avoid reading?

Gathering data about reading behavior at home is more difficult. Some teachers send surveys home asking parents about their child's reading behavior. Such surveys have questionable validity because some parents will not know how much their children read and others may report a level of reading that is inaccurate. Other teachers, especially those in the upper grades, ask students to keep a log of their at-home reading for a couple of weeks.

Independent Reading Level.   Teachers should know the independent reading levels of all their students by administering an IRI. This information is essential to helping children read more. Teachers who know the reading interests and reading levels of their students will have the necessary information to connect children to books they will want to read.

WHAT TEACHERS CAN DO TO PROMOTE INDEPENDENT AND AT-HOME READING

Encouraging Independent Reading in School

I + I: Interesting Books at the Students' Independent Reading Level.   It is not easy to get reluctant readers to read, but your best bet is to remember this formula: Independent reading level + Personal interest = Best chance of success. First, determine the child's independent reading level. Next, either administer an interest survey or ask the student what type of book he or she likes to read. Then, go to the school library or public library and find a book that meets both criteria. This will be a book that the student will be interested in, written at a level he or she can read easily. To get things rolling, it will help if you read the first part of the book to the child.

Sustained Silent Reading (SSR).   SSR is a time when everyone in the classroom reads silently. Held at the same time every day, this may be as little as five minutes a day during the first weeks of Grade 1 to 30 minutes a day in a sixth-grade classroom. Children select their own reading material, which may be books, newspapers, encyclopedias, magazines, or their textbooks. It is very important that everybody, the teacher and any visitors to the room included, read silently. No interruptions are acceptable. SSR is sometimes called DEAR (Drop Everything and Read).

Reader's/Writer's Workshop.   During the height of the Whole Language movement, many teachers used an instructional program format called Reader's Workshop. This was an hour or more a day when children read silently, small groups worked on projects, and the teacher met with individual students and groups of children who shared a similar need. The format was often expanded to include both reading and writing.

A balanced, comprehensive approach to reading instruction makes it difficult for teachers to use reader's/writer's workshop every day. It simply isn't a format conducive to the amount of direct, explicit teaching expected of teachers at the current time. Recently, I have seen teachers with balanced reading programs who use reader's/writer's workshop one or two days a week. This provides time for direct instruction and time for independent reading and writing.

Frequent Opportunities to Share

Children should have many opportunities to talk and write about the books they have read. Sharing reading experiences can motivate children to read more independently.

Literature Logs. As mentioned previously, children should be required to write in their journals responses to books they have read independently. Teachers can provide generic prompts ("Let's write about the setting of the books we are reading independently") or simply say, "Please take out your journal and write something about the book you are reading." The key is that the journals should become interactive—the teacher should write back to the student.

Individual Conferences. There is nothing more valuable than the opportunity to talk to your students in a one-on-one setting. Although many things can be accomplished in an individual conference, such as individual skill and strategy instruction, it is important that the teacher and the student have a conversation about the books the student has read.

Literature Circles, Book Clubs, Response Groups. All of these names refer to the same type of discussion format—a small group of students who are reading the same book, just like the book clubs some adults belong to. They meet occasionally while they read the book and immediately after they have finished. For example, in a fifth-grade classroom, one group is reading *Holes*, another *Ella Enchanted*, and the third, *Bud, Not Buddy*. The teacher's role is to ask questions and to say as little as possible. The questions should be open-ended and provocative in that they have a good chance to spark spirited discussions. Some teachers use a more structured format, assigning roles to students ("moderator," "recorder," etc.) and using a generic set of questions all groups must answer.

PROMOTING BOOKS

In addition to assessing independent student reading and encouraging children to read, teachers must also guide children to high-quality children's books from a wide range of genres written by diverse authors.

Reading Aloud

Almost all elementary school teachers read aloud daily to their students. This is a good way to introduce students to the best of children's literature. Teachers who read aloud effectively, with enthusiasm and dramatic effect, can affect the reading habits of their students. The key is to bring books that are "related" to the read-aloud selection to class. For example, if a teacher is reading aloud *The Runaway Bunny* to a class of first graders, he or she should bring to class other books written by Margaret Wise Brown, like *Goodnight, Moon* and *The Little Island.* A sixth-grade teacher who reads aloud *The Book of Three*, the first book in Lloyd Alexander's five-book series, *The Chronicles of Prydain*, should have copies of the second book in the series, *The Black Cauldron.*

Booktalks

Booktalks are "sales pitches" in which the teacher tries to "sell" students on a book. The teacher displays the book, talks about the characters and setting (without giving away the story, of course), and reads an excerpt. Then, hopefully, some children will want to read the book.

Books Connected to Other Areas of the Curriculum

Teachers should have in the classroom a collection of books (20 to 30) that are connected to units of study in social studies, science, and the arts. This is a good time to encourage children to read information books. For example, a fifth-grade classroom studying Colonial America should have copies of information books such as Edwin Tunis's *Colonial Living* and fiction such as *The Witch of Blackbird Pond* by Elizabeth George Speare.

Trips to the Library

Even in this Information Age, it is important for children to learn how to use the library. Every classroom should have a library of books, containing books at the reading level of every child in the room. All classrooms should regularly visit the school library so children can learn how library books are organized and how to check out books. Each class should annually take a trip to the local public library. Some fortunate schools are within walking distance of public libraries, so monthly "walking" field trips are a possibility. To promote books and independent reading, all children should have public library cards.

SUPPORTING AT-HOME READING

Encourage Kids to Read at Home

A number of variables, of course, make it difficult for teachers to change at-home reading behavior. To encourage children to read at home, teachers can do the following:

Let Children Take Home Books from the Classroom or School Library. Both your classroom and school libraries should have check-out systems so that everyone knows which books a child has borrowed. The vast majority of children will return books promptly. Some children will struggle with returning books and, in those cases, teachers and parents must work together to help children be responsible.

Get Children Excited About Books. I have seen classrooms where a teacher reads aloud the first chapter of a book to a literature study group and the children are so excited they can't wait to get home so they can finish the book. You might review all the ideas

I shared previously about how to encourage independent reading and promote books. Hopefully, your enthusiasm will "spill over" and stimulate at-home reading.

Support Parents

Virtually all parents want their children to become good readers and are willing to work with teachers to support the at-home reading of their children. Here are some ideas to support parents:

Encourage SSR at Home. This requires a high level of parental and sibling support. If SSR time is from 7:30 to 8:00 a.m. on Mondays and Thursdays, this means everybody in the house reads—the phone isn't answered, and the television is turned off.

Provide Lists of Books That Can Be Checked Out of the Public Library. Parents of kindergarteners and first graders welcome a list of books that they can read aloud to their children. Teachers can also prepare lists of books for children to read on their own. I know one teacher who provided each parent with a list of "Fifty Great Books for Fourth Graders." Lists of information books on topics in social studies and science also should be sent home.

Provide Information on the Local Public Library. Teachers can encourage parents to take their children to the public library. A packet should be sent home with maps, times of operation, and information on how to acquire a library card.

Use the First Languages of Your English Learners. Many of our K–12 students have acquired English as a second language. We can support our English Learners (ELs) by acknowledging their bilingual status. All communication with parents should be in the language the parent understands. Parents should be encouraged to read to their children in their native language and, if possible, in English. During SSR at home, it doesn't make any difference which language people read because our goal is the development of the "reading habit." Lists of good books written in a language other than English at public libraries should be made available to parents.

Support Family Literacy Projects. Many elementary schools have established programs to improve the literacy of parents in the community. Although these programs require the expertise of a specialist, classroom teachers can support family literacy projects by disseminating information and supporting parents who participate.

13

Supporting Reading Through Oral and Written Language Development

INTRODUCTION

Our focus in this chapter is the interrelationships among reading, writing, speaking, and listening. Teachers should understand the linkages among the four language arts and how instruction in oral and writing development can enhance reading proficiency. Thus, our purpose will not be to review all aspects of teaching writing, speaking, and listening; we will focus on the assessment of oral and written language development during reading-related activities and instructional activities.

HOW TO ASSESS ORAL AND WRITTEN LANGUAGE

All teachers must be able to assess their students' oral and written language proficiency. The results will serve many purposes, primarily as the foundation for instruction that will help every child develop fully as a speaker and writer. The results of assessments of oral and writing proficiency also can be used to plan reading instruction.

Audience and Purpose

For both oral and written language, audience and purpose should determine the substance and form of what a person says and writes. For example, a shopping list for Saturday's visit to the supermarket will include only sparse descriptions of the items to be purchased, and it may be rather sloppy. The purpose is very limited and the audience is one—the person doing the shopping. On the other hand, an essay written as part of a job application will look quite different. The writer likely will prepare some sort of outline, compose a rough draft, edit, and revise. The final draft will be polished. Thus, the simplest assessment of oral and written language is the answer to the question, "Does the oral comment or written product achieve the speaker's (or writer's) purpose by reaching the speaker's (or writer's) audience?"

Substance and Form

Teachers can assess two aspects of oral and written language: (1) substance and (2) form. Assessments of substance focus on what the student said or wrote; assessments of form focus on how the student said it or wrote it.

For example, for oral language, teachers should gather data to determine whether children "stay on topic." When asked a question, do they provide an answer that is direct and to the point? When they take part in a discussion, do they respond to what others have said or do they bring up extraneous points? When making an oral presentation, have they provided relevant information? These questions get to the substance of their oral comments. The teacher would ask similar questions of the student's writing.

Assessments of the form of oral production focus on choice of words and organization. Are children clear and coherent when they speak? When answering a question, do students emphasize the most relevant points? In discussions and oral presentations, are their comments organized appropriately? In writing, assessment of form focuses on organization and writing mechanics (spelling, punctuation, usage).

Discrete and Holistic

Teachers may assess discrete (or separate) elements of oral language and writing or they may look at a student's commentary or writing as a whole (holistically). For example, if fifth-grade students have written a descriptive, three-paragraph essay on a family activity, the teacher may use discrete analysis and assess the papers only for one element—spelling—or the teacher could look at the essay as a whole and consider all elements of substance and form.

Qualitative and Quantitative

Whether the teacher looks at a single discrete element or the effort as a whole, the teacher's analysis and corresponding response can be either qualitative or quantitative. Qualitative analysis and response is in words. Continuing with our example from the previous section, if the teacher were doing a discrete element analysis of spelling, a qualitative response would be, "Fred, I am pleased that you are spelling more and more words correctly. Hooray for you, you spelled *broccoli* right! The only word you misspelled was hard—*restaurant*." If, on the other hand, the teacher were analyzing the same essay holistically, a qualitative response would be, "Fred, this was an excellent essay. I felt as if I were there at the restaurant with your family. This was your best essay yet!"

When assessing student oral language development, teachers often keep anecdotal records, writing down notes of anything that seems important. This unstructured recording of student performance is qualitative.

Quantitative analysis and response uses numbers to categorize student performance. Continuing with our example, if the teacher read Fred's essay and looked only at spelling, she would give the paper a score, probably something between 1 and 4, based only on his spelling. If the analysis were holistic, then the teacher would use several criteria to assign a single number to Fred's essay, considering his spelling, punctuation, topic sentences, supporting detail, and use of descriptive words.

Teachers will need rubrics if they are using some form of quantitative analysis. The rubrics state criteria and provide descriptors for each category. Please note the rubric can be holistic, based on multiple criteria, or it can be discrete, based on a single element. A well-designed rubric typically has three, four, or five categories. The rubric should provide a clear description of performance in each category. For example, for a descriptive essay to receive the highest score, a 4, the description of a 4 might be: "Essay has few errors in spelling, punctuation, and capitalization. All three paragraphs have topic sentences. The essay provides details of the family experiences and uses descriptive words to provide the reader with a clear picture of the experience."

Assessing Oral Language During Reading-Related Activities

The following reading-related activities can be used to assess oral language development:

Small Group Literature Discussions.   Small group discussions about books provide an ideal opportunity for teachers to gather data on oral language development. Sometimes teachers should take anecdotal notes. This is an effective way to make a record of the "bumps on the horizon"—the events that stand out. For example, a teacher might write the names of students who say nothing. Another time, the teacher might make a record of the comments of a student who was particularly insightful. Teachers should also use discrete element analysis to assess student performance during literature discussion. During a discussion, a teacher might only assess students on a single element, such as, "Does the student listen attentively to others?"

Language Play.   Children in the primary grades will take part in "language play" to develop phonemic awareness and learn the sound-symbol relationships of the English language. Students will chant rhymes, poems, and songs. Teachers should gather data on their oral language development when they do so.

Drama Based on Literature.   Children in all grades should take part in dramatic performances based on children's books. The two most frequently used formats are reader's theater (when children read their lines) and plays. Drama activities provide teachers with opportunities to gather data on the ability of children to (a) learn their parts and (b) change their speaking manner to fit the traits of the characters they are portraying.

Answers to Questions.   During many comprehension-building activities, such as a guided reading lesson, teachers ask students questions about what they have read. The teacher's primary focus, of course, is on the substance of the student's answer. Teachers can also use this opportunity to assess their students' oral language development, especially their ability to summarize information coherently.

Assessing Written Language Development During Reading-Related Activities

Once again, teachers will need to gather data on the substance and form of student writing. As for substance, teachers will ask questions about the content of student-authored essays, stories, and poetry. At the same time, teachers will be concerned about the form of students' writing, particularly the organization and mechanics of written products (spelling, punctuation, capitalization).

Teachers should keep portfolios of student writing. Their contents will enable teachers to see the longitudinal growth of their students. A portfolio is a place of storage and may be as simple as a manila folder. Most teachers will allow students to select their own favorite pieces for inclusion in the portfolio, along with pieces of writing the teacher wants to save.

All of the following reading-related activities can be used to make evaluations about student writing development:

- Journals with responses to literature
- Stories based on the characters, setting, theme, or style of a book
- Answers to questions written as part of reading lessons
- Essays about issues and themes raised in books
- Captions to illustrations from books

HOW TO TEACH: INTEGRATING ORAL LANGUAGE DEVELOPMENT AND READING

Reading-related oral language activities challenge students to talk in ways that meet their purpose and reach their audience. Here are some reading-related oral language activities that teachers should implement with their students:

Language Play to Develop Phonics and Phonemic Awareness

Language play includes chants, rhymes, poems, and songs—anything that focuses on the sounds of words. These activities will develop phonemic awareness and can help children understand the sound-symbol relationships of English. Most of these oral activities are done in choral fashion (more than one child talks at a time).

Drama

Good literature should serve as the basis for dramatic projects in the elementary classroom. Entire books, parts of books, and abridgements of books can be used as the script for plays and reader's theater presentations (remember, in reader's theater, the child-actors read their parts). Dramatic projects demand a different kind of oral proficiency than that required by conversation or classroom recitation. Children must adapt their speaking manner to fit the characters they are portraying.

Group Discussions of Books

Small group discussions provide children with excellent opportunities to develop their oral proficiency. Children will learn how to speak clearly and concisely, how to be good listeners, how to take turns, and how to respond to the comments of others. Children's literature provides the topics for these conversations.

The groups should be small, from three to six members. The teacher plays several roles. At first, he or she should model good group conversation skills (i.e., by disagreeing without being disagreeable—"That's a good point, Fred, and I agree with most of what you said, but I think . . . "). Ultimately, the teacher becomes a facilitator, saying as little as possible to keep the conversation going.

Children should learn the rules of productive group discussions: (1) don't interrupt; (2) don't dominate; (3) address ideas, not people; (4) clarify others' comments; (5) expand on others' comments; and (6) state your perspectives clearly and support them with details.

Answering Questions

While and after children read, typically as part of a guided reading lesson, teachers will ask them to answer questions. This is an excellent way to help children develop the ability to "think on their feet." Answers to higher-level comprehension questions (inference, cause-effect relationships, generalizing, and evaluating) will challenge students to think critically before they express themselves.

Sharing Content Information After Content-Area Reading

Students will read content-area texts to gather information (once again, content-area material includes social studies textbooks, science textbooks, encyclopedias, and Internet sites). Although the traditional oral report can be a boring experience for all, many teachers help children develop their formal oral presentation skills by teaching their students how to organize what they are going to say and to use visual aids to support the message.

HOW TO TEACH: WRITTEN LANGUAGE DEVELOPMENT AND READING

The Writing Process

Many reading-related activities will help children become more proficient in each phase of the writing process. For example, after students have read E. B. White's *Stuart Little*, they may write a sequel describing Stuart's further adventures. While some writing tasks do not require the use of each stage of the writing process (such as writing a grocery list), most writing tasks do. Here is a quick summary of the writing process:

Stage One: Pre-Writing. Here, students choose or narrow their topic. They should learn how to consider their purpose and audience before deciding on the form of the final written product. Children will generate main ideas and organize supporting detail. This can be accomplished by making a semantic web (cluster), talking to classmates, doing a "quick write," drawing a picture, or writing an outline.

Stage Two: Drafting. Using the pre-writing product as a basis, the student composes a first draft.

Stage Three: Revising/Editing. During this phase, someone needs to edit the first draft. The editor can be the writer herself, a teacher, or classmates. The writer then makes revisions based on the editor's suggestions.

Stage Four: Final Draft. Usually the revision completed in stage three will be the final draft. For some pieces of writing, however, multiple copies of a final draft will be made for multiple readers.

Journals

As part of experiences with literature and with content-area texts, elementary school children will write in journals. Journal writing is informal. The journals themselves can be composition books or simply paper in a folder. Experiences with high-quality children's books in particular can be used as a basis for each of the following types of journals:

Personal Journals. Personal journals are private and should be read only by the student and the teacher.

Dialogue Journals. In this type of journal, the entries are meant to be shared. A classmate or the teacher reads the entries in the journal and then writes a response.

Reading Logs/Reader Response Journals. In this category, students record the date they begin and the date they finish reading a book. As they read the book, intermediate-level and older students write journal entries, noting how characters or events make them feel. All students complete their journal entries by writing about the book after they finish reading it.

Double-Entry Journals. Students divide each journal page in half. One kind of information is written on one side and another type of information is written on the other half. An example is "quotes and notes," a type of double-entry journal in which the student writes a direct quote from a book and then a response.

Content Learning Logs. This type of journal is used in social studies and science. Students write down questions they want answered, copy assignments, and list important information they have learned.

Writing Stories

Experiences with children's books can serve as the basis for creative writing experiences. Once they have learned about story grammars, story frames, and story maps, children can use these devices during the pre-writing phase of the writing process. Our youngest children may need to start by first creating the illustrations and then writing the text to their stories.

Literature and Modes (or Genres) of Writing

Through their experiences with literature, older students can learn to write in many different modes, also called written *genres*. These modes include forms of poetry, ABC books, fairy tales, myths, mysteries, and science fiction.

Expository Modes

Finally, children need to become proficient in writing expository (informational) text. Experiences with content-area material will help children see the difference between expository and narrative (stories) texts. Some of the expository modes that children should be taught to write include brief descriptions of persons, places, or events; friendly letters; formal letters; summaries with main ideas and supporting details; persuasive letters; and reports based on information gathered from several sources. Expository writing might require students to use expository text patterns and include writing about cause-and-effect relationships; writing about a problem and its solution; comparing or contrasting concepts, ideas, or events; sequencing events; and writing content descriptions and supporting these descriptions with details and examples.

Our Youngest Writers

Our youngest writers, kindergarteners and first graders, will complete a variety of written assignments, each with the goal of helping them master the intricacies of writing in English.

Writing Each Letter of the Alphabet. When teachers teach students to recognize the 26 letters of the English alphabet, they should, at the same time, teach them to write the letters.

Interactive or Shared Writing. Children's literature can serve as the basis for many interactive writing experiences. Interactive writing is an instructional format in which children and their teacher create a text together—actually sharing the pen as the text is written on a piece of chart paper or an overhead projector. The teacher and the children compose together.

Language Experience Approach. This is a good activity for showing children that their ideas can be preserved through writing (see Chapter 3, "Concepts About Print," for a description).

Captions for Illustrations. This is an excellent beginning writing activity. Young children draw a picture and first dictate a caption. Then, at some point, they write the caption themselves.

14 Structure of the English Language

INTRODUCTION

"Structure of the English language" refers to the rules for the use of written English. Students' knowledge of the structure of English is essential if they are to become competent writers. In addition, knowledge of the rules of English can help students become better readers, especially by promoting reading fluency and comprehension. This area includes the following: (1) sentence structure, (2) rules of English usage, (3) punctuation, and (4) capitalization. These aspects of language have, at times, been referred to as *grammar* or *written English language conventions*.

DEFINITIONS

The topics mentioned in the previous paragraph have for many years been referred to as "teaching grammar." Educators do not share a common definition for *grammar*. Linguists define it as a description of a language, including the sound system of that language (phonology), the system of creating words (morphology), the rules for forming sentences (syntax), and the nuances of word meaning (semantics). For our purposes, the word *grammar* means the rules of English. It is a broad term that includes sentence structure, punctuation, capitalization, and usage.

Sentence structure refers to the rules of composing correct sentences in English. Not all combinations of words are correct and form sentences. For example, *The Oakland Raiders are going to win the Super Bowl this year* is an acceptable sentence in English. *Raiders are Super Bowl year this win to the Oakland the going* is not. A number of things can be taught as a part of sentence structure: subject and predicate; incomplete and run-on sentences; simple, compound, and complex sentences; and independent and dependent clauses.

A *clause* has a subject and a predicate. A clause that can stand alone as an acceptable sentence is an *independent clause* (e.g., *Darlene kicked the ball*). On the other hand, a clause that is not a complete thought is a *dependent clause* (e.g., in the sentence *Darlene kicked the ball to Fred, who kicked it to Allen*, the dependent clause is *who kicked it to Allen*).

A *simple sentence* has one independent clause (*Mr. Elgourach saw the white flag*). A *compound sentence* is made up of two or more independent clauses (*He felt that he would be short forever, and he tried to get used to it*). *Complex sentences* have one independent and one or more dependent clauses (*When he was awake, he was happy and sad at the same time*).

Usage refers to correctness, or using the appropriate word or phrase in a sentence. In English, rules of proper usage vary with each dialect. Just think of all the appropriate ways of saying certain phrases in London, England, that are different from the way we say certain phrases in Los Angeles, California! Also, rules of usage vary with each situation. Choices of words and phrasing should be different, for example, if you are addressing the California Supreme Court or if you are talking to friends while watching a NASCAR race.

Examples of improper usage include using *catched* instead of *caught*; double subjects (*My mom she is a system analyst*); *hisself* for *himself*; or selecting the wrong pronoun (*Me and my friend went to the store*).

Punctuation marks and capital letters are two items that make written English different from spoken English. They must be used appropriately in written English, but they are inferred by the listener in spoken English.

HOW TO ASSESS THE STRUCTURE
OF THE ENGLISH LANGUAGE

Samples of Student Writing

The most valid sources of information about a student's knowledge of sentence structure, rules of usage, punctuation, and capitalization are the written texts a student produces during the school year. In other words, the real test is what students write. Thus, it is important for teachers to review and analyze the journal entries, stories, and essays students write. This type of assessment must be ongoing, and conclusions should be reached only after analyzing multiple pieces of student writing.

Teachers should use rubrics to organize their analysis (this was covered in Chapter 13, "Supporting Reading Through Oral and Written Language Development"). Again, teachers can analyze a piece of writing using multiple criteria (capitalization, punctuation) or a single criterion (proper sentence structure with no run-on sentences or sentence fragments).

Tests

Almost all of us have experienced tests of our knowledge of the structure of the English language. Most standardized tests of student achievement include a test of sentence structure, usage, punctuation, and capitalization. Most language arts textbook series have tests for students. Teachers can develop their own tests, but again, it is important to note that no test is a substitute for analyzing student writing. Some of the testing formats include:

- **The scrambled paragraph.** Students are confronted with a paragraph containing sentences out of order. They must put them in the proper order.
- **Error analysis.** Students are presented with sentences that have been divided into four or five parts. One part of the sentence contains an error such as incorrect usage or missing punctuation. Students must identify the part of the sentence that is incorrect.
- **Choice of words.** A word is missing in a sentence. To test knowledge of usage, students are presented with two or more choices (e.g., *who* or *whom*) to fill in the missing word.

HOW TO TEACH THE STRUCTURE OF THE ENGLISH LANGUAGE

There are significant differences of opinion about how to best teach the structure of the English language. There are disagreements over how much time should be devoted to this, or what precisely should be taught, or when certain topics should be covered. Questions of what and when have been resolved, to a large degree, by the English or language arts standards adopted in each state. We will discuss how to use direct and explicit instruction.

Direct Lessons

Much of what has been presented so far regarding the direct teaching of reading skills and strategies applies to the direct teaching of English language structure. It is important to assess students' needs. For example, a fourth-grade teacher likely will have many students who understand the use of question marks; he needs only to teach a direct lesson on their use to those children who do not use them appropriately in their written work.

Teachers can choose from many resources—lessons on the structure of English are in basal reader workbooks and in the language arts textbooks that most school districts have purchased for classroom use.

A whole-part-whole approach would seem to work best when teaching sentence structure, punctuation, capitalization, parts of speech, and rules of English usage. For example, if the objective of a lesson is to teach students that the contraction *aren't* means *are not*, then the teacher should start by displaying sentences such as *Terri and Sonia aren't sisters but they look alike* and *Rich Harden and Barry Zito aren't members of the San Francisco Giants; they play for the Oakland A's.* The teacher would isolate the target contraction, circling *aren't* in each sentence. Then the teacher would explain that *aren't* is an abbreviated form of *are not.* After that, students would generate new sentences using *aren't.*

Individual Conferences

Teachers should have regular conferences with each student in their classroom to review the contents of the student's writing portfolio. Although the primary purpose of these conferences is to talk about the substance of what the student has written, teachers should also use the opportunity to teach mini-lessons on the structure of the English language. For example, a second-grade teacher notices that a student continues to produce run-on sentences. The individual conference is a good time to show the child how to rewrite his work to include proper end punctuation.

Error Analysis

Many elementary school teachers use some kind of daily exercise to analyze grammatically incorrect sentences. On the blackboard, the teacher displays a sentence containing three or four errors. Students are then challenged to rewrite the sentence correctly. This is a good way for children to review what they have learned about the structure of the English language.

Language Activities to Build Knowledge of Academic Language

Teachers should plan and implement a variety of activities to help students master the use of "academic" language—the way of speaking and writing in school and most business settings.

Model.   First, it is important that teachers continually provide a model of acceptable English usage when they speak and write.

Reading Aloud Content-Area Texts.   Most teachers select narrative texts to read aloud to children (novels, picture book stories). To provide a model of expository text structures to children, teachers should read aloud from biographies, information books, social studies and science textbooks, newspapers, and magazines.

Sentence Expansion and Combining.   In a sentence expansion activity, children are challenged to lengthen simple sentences. For example, the teacher writes the following sentence on the board: *The firefighter ran.* Then, the teacher asks students to describe the firefighter (*The tall, strong firefighter ran*). Next, the teacher asks the students to consider why, where, and when the action is taking place (*The tall, strong firefighter ran into the burning building after she heard a person screaming*).

A sentence-combining activity involves combining two simple sentences into a compound sentence. For example, the teacher presents two sentences to her students: *Kerry Collins threw a pass to Randy Moss. Randy Moss ran to the 10-yard line.* The students would work to combine the sentences into one. (There are many possibilities, such as *Kerry Collins threw a pass to Randy Moss, who ran to the 10-yard line.*)

Direct Vocabulary Teaching.   Some words need to be taught directly, using the strategies described in Chapter 9. For example, you will need to teach words that are frequently used in academic settings, such as *compare, contrast, cause, effect, analyze,* and *synthesize.*

Proofreading

Finally, another instructional activity that will help students enhance their understanding of the structure of the English language is proofreading. This is a significant challenge because students must apply what they have learned about sentence structure, punctuation, capitalization, and the rules of English usage. Students should be asked to proofread both their own work and papers written by classmates. It probably is best to start with a proofreading exercise requiring an analysis for just one type of error (e.g., just look for punctuation errors).

15

English Learners

INTRODUCTION

English Learners (ELs) are children whose first language is not English. Most ELs are acquiring English as a second language, though there are ELs who will acquire English as a third or fourth language. Previously, these children were described as students of Limited English Proficiency (LEPs). The descriptor EL, or English Language Learner (ELL), is now more widely used. Demographic patterns in the United States have resulted in a student population that is diverse in regard to language status. In my home state, California, over one-third of our K–12 students are ELs. There are ELs in every state in the union, with increasing populations in areas that until recently have had very few ELs (e.g., Illinois and North Carolina). Teachers need to know a great deal about how to help ELs acquire English proficiency in speaking, listening, reading, and writing. Given the scope of this book, our view here is limited. We review what teachers should know and be able to do to help their ELs learn to read in English.

Our discussion looks at three topics: (1) appropriate reading experiences for ELs at each stage of English proficiency, (2) the elements of "sheltered reading instruction," and (3) the factors and processes involved in transferring reading ability in another language to reading in English.

READING EXPERIENCES AT EACH STAGE OF ENGLISH PROFICIENCY

From the outset, it is important to note that there is a big difference in teaching ELs who are literate in their first language and teachng ELs who have not acquired first-language literacy. In this section, we are assuming little or no first-language literacy. Effective instruction of ELs is aligned to their level of English proficiency. This is crucial for English reading instruction. Although there are many other possible classification systems, we will use the following levels of oral English proficiency: preproduction, early production, speech emergent, intermediate fluency.

Preproduction

English Learners at this stage listen and may utter a few words. Children rely, for the most part, on gestures and their first language. This stage can last from a few hours to a few weeks. Reading-related activities and lessons include:

- Teach certain "survival" words, such as *boys, girls, stop.* Teach children to read and write their names and addresses in English. There are limits to English literacy instruction with ELs at the preproduction stage. Teachers should focus on listening and speaking.

Early Production

In this stage, children acquiring English begin to utter single words and short phrases. This stage can last for a long time, perhaps as long as nine months. Reading-related activities and lessons include:

- English concepts about print can now be taught. Early Production ELs need to understand the directionality of English and the difference between English letters and words. They can learn the names of the English letters and how to write them. (Don't forget: ELs who have learned to read in their first language already have acquired many of these concepts.)
- Children at this stage will enjoy listening to their teacher read aloud simple English picture books.
- ELs can be encouraged to join in during choral readings of rhymes and chants.
- Regarding phonemic awareness and phonics, Early Production ELs can begin to recognize and speak English phonemes that correspond to phonemes they hear in their native language. They can begin to learn the letters that English uses to represent these common sounds.
- Children need to begin to build their sight vocabulary, focusing on high-frequency words. Vocabulary lessons should focus on objects commonly found in classrooms and everyday locations (food markets).
- Comprehension instruction begins with several activities. Children can be asked to describe events they see pictured in books, although the responses will be single words and short phrases. They can be expected to follow two- and three-step oral instructions.
- Early Production ELs can begin to write by labeling illustrations.

Speech Emergent

Now ELs have progressed to a stage where their speech is more readily understood. They speak in sentences and are able to describe events and experiences. Conversation with native English speakers is now more productive. ELs can begin to write meaningful units of text and read books with limited vocabularies. Reading-related activities and lessons include:

- Children at this stage of English proficiency are ready to tackle more challenging literacy activities. They need to continue to master English phonics, working on consonants, long and short vowels, and the most common rimes.
- Many lessons should focus on the meanings of words, and Speech Emergent children can benefit from lessons on the most common prefixes and suffixes. Students at this level can also be challenged to recognize cognates and false cognates between their first language and English. Cognates are pairs of words from different languages that look and sound the same and, in fact, mean the same thing in both languages (e.g,, Spanish *agonía* and *agony*). False cognates look the same, but mean different things (e.g., Spanish *éxito* and *exit*).
- The child's sight vocabulary should greatly expand to include many words from social studies and science.
- The Language Experience Approach can be used with children at this stage. However, ELs at this stage should be encouraged to write in English. Speech Emergent children can begin to write in journals.

- ELs at this stage will benefit from well-designed, sheltered comprehension lessons (see the next section). As with all students, the focus should be on question classification/answer verification, strategic reading, and story structure. Speech Emergent children can complete story maps, story grammars, and story frames.
- Many books can now be read independently. Speech Emergent children need to be encouraged to read self-selected books silently.

Intermediate Fluency

At this stage, students have achieved a high level of oral proficiency. The real challenges now are in literacy and being able to read grade-level textbooks in social studies and science. Reading-related activities and lessons include:

- Students will have mastered the sound-symbol relationships of English. Now is the time to work on advanced word analysis skills, such as understanding the more difficult prefixes and suffixes and Greek and Latin roots.
- Vocabulary instruction can be more challenging. Students need to learn that many English words have more than one meaning.
- The main focus of vocabulary teaching, however, is on "academic language": words needed to write and read in the content areas.
- The great challenge here is helping English Learners complete difficult reading and writing assignments in social studies and science. Content-area reading lessons should make use of graphic organizers, study guides, and data retrieval charts. The sheltered strategies described in the following section are essential. ELs at this stage need to be taught how to write well-constructed essays.

SHELTERED READING INSTRUCTION

The key concept here is that teachers need to provide scaffolding for reading lessons with ELs. A scaffold is some instructional intervention that assists the student in learning. This is the same concept as sheltered instruction in social studies or science: The teacher builds the learning scaffold so that the EL achieves the same objectives as everybody else. (In California, this type of instruction is called Specially Designed Academic Instruction in English—SDAIE.)

Instructional Interventions

Teachers can support the reading development of their ELs by selecting any or all of the following interventions:

Differentiated Vocabulary Instruction: Visual Aids and Real Objects. All the vocabulary methods described in Chapter 9 can help ELs. With ELs, a picture is worth a thousand words. Even better than a photograph or illustration, however, would be to use real objects to teach essential vocabulary before children read (i.e., to teach the meaning of *asparagus*, the best thing a teacher can do is to allow students to handle real asparagus while the teacher gives the students the words to identify and describe it).

Differentiated Vocabulary Instruction: Additional Words. If you are teaching a content-area reading lesson using a chapter from your social studies textbook, you might have identified five key words to teach before students are asked to read. For lessons with ELs, the relevant question is, "Are there additional words in the reading assignment that might confuse my English Learners?" Take special note of any idiomatic phrases. Idioms are phrases that cannot be understood even if you know the meaning of each word (e.g., "It is raining cats and dogs").

Preview-Review.   A preview of the lesson, including the objective, is given in the student's first language. After the lesson, a review of what was learned is provided in the first language. Obviously, this requires a teacher, aide, or student helper who is bilingual.

Graphic Organizers/Outlines.   Graphic organizers (see Chapter 10, "Content-Area Literacy") or a simple outline displayed before ELs read will help them activate their background knowledge and predict what they are about to read.

Charts.   For highlighting essential information in a text, charts work better for ELs than other types of study guides. In content-area reading lessons, ELs do well with data retrieval charts. With stories, story grammars, story maps, and story frames can help English Learners.

Teacher Model/Explicit Instruction.   Two instructional practices will help ELs during reading lessons. First, it is important that teachers model any behavior they want students to do themselves. If, for example, a word is to be circled on a workbook page, then the teacher should make a plastic transparency of the page and demonstrate on the overhead projector the drawing of a circle around the correct answer. Second, teachers should be absolutely clear when they ask ELs to do something. Lessons with a single objective and simple-to-follow instructions will increase the ELs' chances of being successful.

TRANSFERRING READING ABILITY IN ANOTHER LANGUAGE TO ENGLISH

English and Other Writing Systems

Some knowledge of the written forms of English and other writing systems is essential if you are to understand the factors and processes of learning to read in English after you have learned to read in another language. English is an alphabetic system. In an alphabetic system, letters represent sounds. Some other languages are alphabetic but do not use the same 26 letters as English. In Greece, for example, people use the Greek alphabet:

Α Β Γ Δ Ε Ζ Η Θ Ι Κ Λ Μ Ν Ξ Ο Π Ρ Σ Τ Υ Φ Χ Ψ Ω

And in Ukraine, people use the Cyrillic alphabet:

А Б В Г Д Е Ё Ж З И Й К Л М Н О П Р С Т У Ф Х Ц Ч Ш Щ Ъ Ы Ь Э Ю Я

Among alphabetic languages, some authorities classify language according to the regularity of sound-symbol languages. Languages that have a high degree of regularity (Spanish, Italian) are called *transparent*. Languages with more complex sound-symbol relationships (French, English) are *opaque*.

Chinese, on the other hand, is a logographic system. Symbols represent words (actually, in linguistic terms, the symbols represent morphemes). In a logographic system there are thousands of symbols.

Generally speaking, the closer the first language resembles English, the easier it will be to transfer the first-language reading ability to reading English. Thus, going from an alphabetic system with an orthography similar to English (e.g., German or Spanish) to English will be easier than going from an orthography that is different (e.g., Russian). Most difficult will be making the transfer from a logographic language to English.

What Transfers from Another Language to English

If children have learned to read in their first language, there is much they can transfer to learning to read English.

Concepts About Print.   ELs who have learned to read in their first language will have acquired several concepts about print. They will have the general idea that print carries meaning, and that concept is the most important of all. They will know the parts of books. They may also have acquired the sense of directionality of printed texts (assuming that their first language moves left to right, top to bottom, as in English). Regardless of what language the child first reads, he or she will have a good understanding of what "reading is all about," unlike children who have had little or no exposure to reading and writing.

Word Identification.   Children who have learned to read in an alphabetic language will have the alphabetic principle—that letters represent sounds. A child moving from a transparent language (Spanish) to an opaque one (English) may be amazed at the complexity of English sound-symbol relationships. ELs who learned to read in a logographic language will need to be taught the alphabetic principle. Please note that initially literate ELs will apply their knowledge of their first language sound-symbol relationships to English. Children who have learned to read in German, for example, most likely will think the English *w* makes the /*v*/ sound. Most difficult for any EL are the sounds that exists in English that do not exist in his or her first language. It may take a great deal of time for the EL to utter these sounds.

Vocabulary.   If the EL's first language belongs to the Romance family (French, Italian, Portuguese, Romanian, or Spanish) or the Germanic family of languages (German, Dutch, Swedish, etc.), then there is a good chance that some English vocabulary has already been learned because the English word is similar to the same word in the student's first language. As noted previously, lessons on cognates and false cognates are essential for English Learners.

Comprehension.   Older ELs who have achieved advanced literacy in their first language will have acquired all three levels of reading comprehension skills: literal, inferential, and evaluative. Likewise, there is a very good chance that these older ELs with high levels of first-language literacy will know how to read strategically. They know how to predict, summarize, clarify, and generate questions. These ELs know how to think critically. These abilities don't need to be retaught, though it will take time before the EL can use them while reading English.

Reading Habits and Behaviors.   Children who have learned to read in their first language will have acquired certain habits and behaviors that will help them become literate in English. For example, they will know that some texts must be read silently, which requires a quiet time and a quiet place. ELs who can read well in their first language probably know about libraries—how to check books out and how to behave there.

Some of you are using this book to study for a comprehensive examination on reading instruction. Many states now require this type of "high-stakes exit" exam. This chapter proposes strategies that will help you pass that type of test.

1. DON'T WASTE TIME "SELF-ASSESSING" BECAUSE YOU DON'T HAVE TO GET EVERY ANSWER RIGHT TO PASS THE TEST

Find out what the passing score is on the test you will take. In most cases, the threshold is set rather low, sometimes around 70%. This means you don't have to answer every question right to pass the test. If this is so, the following two thoughts should not enter your head: "Hey, I'm doing great on this test," or "Oh my gosh, I'm going to fail." *Don't waste your time evaluating your performance.* Your attitude when you take the test should be very businesslike. Just answer the questions.

2. BUDGET YOUR TIME

Most comprehensive reading examinations are timed. One reason some people fail is *not* lack of knowledge. Rather, it is not budgeting the time spent on each question. In most cases, there will be information either on a Web site or in the test registration bulletin that will tell you how many questions there will be on the test and how long you have to complete it. You should do the math and allocate your time. For example, if there are 80 multiple choice questions and you have 90 minutes to complete them, then you know you only can spend about one minute on each question. If there are 10 essay questions and you have two hours (120 minutes), then allocate 12 minutes for each question.

Be sure you have a watch when you take the exam and budget your time!

3. DEVELOP A STRATEGY FOR COMPLETING THE MULTIPLE CHOICE SECTION

Don't get bogged down or frustrated on the multiple choice section of the exam. Unless the examination you take has a unique format, there will be many more multiple choice questions than essay tasks. It is a mistake to spend nine or ten minutes agonizing over one multiple choice question. You will have done the math; you will know how long you can take on each multiple choice question. Be strict with yourself.

Find out how the multiple choice section is scored. On many tests, there is no penalty for guessing, so answer every question even if you are not sure of the correct response. On the other hand, if the multiple choice section is scored in a fashion that accounts for incorrect responses, then you would not want to guess wildly. Again, find out how the multiple choice section is scored.

Be sure you read every answer option carefully. First eliminate any answer options that are clearly wrong. Then, carefully consider your remaining choices. Select the best possible answer, realizing that sometimes a correct answer will not "leap out" at you.

4. DEVELOP AN APPROPRIATE STRATEGY FOR ANSWERING THE ESSAYS

Stay Within the Word-Count Boundaries

Find out how long your answers should be (100 words? 300 words?) and stick to those limits. Too many students confuse quantity with quality. Almost all reading tests have scoring rubrics for each essay. The evaluators will be looking to see if your response includes certain things. They will not be impressed by a lengthy answer that does not respond to the question.

Write Legibly

Don't expect the person reading your essays to read your essays over and over again to try to figure out what you wrote.

Answer Each Part of the Question

Be sure to answer each part of the question if the question has multiple parts. For example, the California reading exam—the Reading Instruction Competence Assessment (RICA)—has a Web site with a sample essay question that has these three parts:

(1) Identify one comprehension need demonstrated by Amie (the student in the scenario presented in the question).

To answer this part of the question, simply write a sentence that clearly states Amie's area of need *and cite* the evidence in the question that you relied on to reach that conclusion.

(2) Describe an instructional strategy or activity to help address this need.

In this part of your answer, be sure to tell the reader precisely what the teacher and the student will do. Be specific. Don't just write something like "implement a direct, explicit lesson on how to predict a story's outcome." Write three or four sentences describing the activity. Also, if you mention a specific instructional approach, like Reciprocal Teaching, do not assume the reader shares your understanding of that approach. Again, take the time to write three or four sentences describing what the teacher and the student will be doing.

(3) Explain why the strategy or activity you describe would be effective.

A portion of a question that asks you to explain why something works is asking for a rationale. How does the strategy help the student? Do not continue to describe what is going on. You could mention the particular strengths of the approach, or you could cite a theoretical or research foundation.

Use Subtitles

I suggest you use subtitles to structure your essay. Make it easy for the person grading your essay to figure out what part of the question you are answering. For the example provided above, your answer should have three clearly labeled subtitles:

(1) One Reading Comprehension Need

(2) An Instructional Strategy or Activity to Address That Need

(3) Why the Strategy or Activity Would Be Effective

Under each subtopic you would write an appropriate number of sentences to fully answer the question.

Budget Your Time

And, yes, you must stay within the time allotments you have calculated for each essay question!

5. FIND OUT AS MUCH AS YOU CAN ABOUT THE TEST YOU WILL TAKE

Is there a Web site for the test? Many state reading instruction exams have excellent Web sites with sample exam questions. Try to find an outline of the test's content, sometimes called *content specifications*. A test's content specifications usually are available on the test's Web site. Be careful about relying on the comments made by fellow students who have taken the test. For one thing, many of these tests require test-takers to sign agreements not to discuss the test for several years. These requirements should be taken seriously. Finally, comments by previous test-takers provide little useful guidance, because most reading instruction exams have several forms, and there is little chance you will take the same form of the test that someone took earlier.

The sample test at the end of this book has two short essay and two long essay questions. The answer section provides examples of good responses to the essays.

Sample Examination

You have four hours (240 minutes) to complete this examination.

MULTIPLE CHOICE SECTION

Select the correct answer for each question.

1. **A first-grade teacher reads aloud to her students at least twice a day. Though she sometimes reads information books and poetry, she usually reads picture storybooks. She feels this will help her students develop:**
   a. An understanding of story structure
   b. An understanding of the proper spellings for diphthongs, like the *oi* in *oil*
   c. Left to right directionality
   d. All concepts about print

2. **Mr. Niyongabo teaches kindergarten. A reading specialist who works at his school reviewed his instructional program and saw that he had not planned shared book experiences. Mr. Niyongabo can't wait to plan his first shared book experience. What is the first thing he will need to do?**
   a. Get plenty of writing paper with clearly marked lines
   b. Write each of the words on Fry's New Instant Word List on 3 × 5-inch cards
   c. Find some big books
   d. Rearrange the furniture in his room

3. **Ms. Garcia teaches first grade. She has become frustrated with her attempts to use the Language Experience Approach (LEA) with her students. She uses the LEA with some of her students in Spanish, which is their first language. For her English speakers, she uses the LEA in English. She is frustrated because her students don't seem to say very much. Thus, she has little to write. This could be because:**
   a. For almost all of the LEA sessions, she insists on selecting the topics; for example, yesterday's topic was "Why should we work together to keep our classroom clean?"
   b. Her students have not mastered the initial consonant sound-symbol relationships
   c. Her students speak very little English
   d. She doesn't use 10 × 14-inch newsprint paper with room at the top of each sheet for her students to illustrate what they have dictated

4. **Ms. Griffith teaches kindergarten. She wants to help her students understand that print carries meaning, so she has decided to construct a learning center**

featuring examples of environmental print. She will include all of the following except:
   a. Old cereal boxes
   b. Big books
   c. Bumper stickers
   d. Candy wrappers

5. **Mr. Ribiero is a fifth-grade teacher. Almost all of his students are excellent readers. He has four students, however, who have difficulty understanding what they read despite the fact that they make very few word identification errors. To help this group of four students, he could:**
   a. Develop a comprehensive plan to teach meaning vocabulary, especially key words this group of students will encounter in their basal readers and social studies and science textbooks
   b. Assess the students to determine if each has developed phonemic awareness; if not, he should begin with a series of lessons on sound matching
   c. Teach students to use guide words when they are using the dictionary
   d. Do very little; there is every reason to believe that this group of children will "outgrow" the problem with little help

6. **Ms. Junxia teaches fifth grade. She has five students who have difficulty with end punctuation. When they write, they sometimes omit any ending mark. More frequently they use a period to end all sentences, even those requiring a question mark or an exclamation point. She has decided to teach this group of children a series of five lessons on end punctuation. Knowledge of the proper use of end punctuation affects reading performance because:**
   a. Students who know how to use end punctuation appropriately will make fewer errors when asked to make up words with many prefixes and suffixes
   b. Not all languages use the same end punctuation as English
   c. End punctuation is one aspect of knowing the structure of the English language
   d. It will help students understand the meaning of the text

7. **Mr. White wants to do a better job of teaching meaning vocabulary. He realizes that there are many words in the English language that his fifth graders don't know. Which words should he select for his meaning vocabulary lessons?**
   a. Words that are topically related to each other and words needed to comprehend a reading selection
   b. The best idea is to proceed in alphabetical order: First, teach words that begin with *A,* then proceed to words that begin with *B*
   c. Words the children are most interested in learning
   d. Start by teaching the meanings of the words his students already know because that will help them learn key strategies for learning words they don't know

8. **Ms. Young is a first-grade teacher. Six of her students are having difficulty learning the corresponding sounds that go with the consonants at the end of words. The first thing she should do for these students is:**

a. Begin planning a series of direct, explicit lessons that will teach them consonant blends and consonant digraphs

b. Administer a test of concepts about print

c. Decide whether or not it is important for this group of children to be taught phonics

d. Do a thorough assessment to see if they can hear the individual sounds that occur at the end of words

9. **Ms. Strober is a fourth-grade teacher. She has five English Learners. She wants to help them learn to read in English. She should:**

   a. Conduct daily assessments of each EL's word identification skills

   b. Not teach directionality and tracking of print if her English Learners know how to read in Spanish

   c. Understand that if the children have learned to read in a language other than English, there will be a negative transfer of those literacy skills to English

   d. Place these students in the same group for comprehension lessons

10. **Ms. Barrios is the principal at Shangri La School. Recent test results showed that students at her school did poorly on phonics tasks. The primary-grade teachers at her school agree that something must be done. As a first step, Ms. Barrios should suggest that her teachers do which of the following?**

    a. Teach the rules of sound-symbol relationships by requiring children to restate those rules in language appropriate for their level of development

    b. Work more on prefixes and suffixes, with emphasis on prefixes that negate (like *un-*, *non-*)

    c. Conduct a thorough assessment of each child to determine precisely which sound-symbol relationships each child knows and does not know

    d. Ask students more questions that require critical thinking, using materials designed for first, second, and third graders

11. **Ms. Chung sang, "Who has the /m/ word to share with us?" as her students looked at the stuffed animals she gave them. Fred, who had a monkey, said, "I do, Ms. Chung!" This is an example of:**

    a. A child who can successfully do sound identity tasks and is developing phonemic awareness

    b. Automaticity, in this case, automaticity of memory

    c. A teacher who facilitates reading comprehension before students read, while they read, and after they read

    d. A phonics lesson that is highly motivational

12. **Ms. Keino is a fourth-grade teacher. She wants to increase the meaning vocabularies of her students. In addition to teaching her students the meanings of difficult words they will read in their basal readers, social studies textbooks, and science textbooks, Ms. Keino should also:**

    a. Begin to use a direct and explicit approach to phonics

    b. Be sure that each student completes at least one workbook page a week

c. Do what is necessary to increase both the amount of time her students read and the types of books they read

d. Assess all her students for their ability to distinguish simple, compound, and complex sentences

13. **A teacher who wants to increase the amount of time students spend reading independently has many possible instructional interventions to consider. If a teacher considers the possibilities and decides to administer an informal reading inventory (IRI), what is the rationale behind this choice?**

   a. An IRI has a high degree of validity because the inventory will include a battery of tests, each allowing the teacher to view reading development from a different perspective

   b. In order to help children select books that are written at a level they can easily understand, it will be necessary to determine each child's independent reading level

   c. Research shows that the amount of time any child spends reading independently depends on many factors

   d. Student independent reading plays a critical role in promoting students' familiarity with language patterns

14. **Mr. Serdula teaches fifth grade. He has a student, Fred, who needs to increase his meaning vocabulary. Fred seems to learn the meanings of the words Mr. Serdula directly teaches. Fred, however, "falls apart" when he comes to a word he does not know when he is reading independently. Mr. Serdula should:**

   a. Teach Fred the meanings of common prefixes and suffixes

   b. Give Fred the responsibility of creating the semantic feature analysis charts that Mr. Serdula will use in his lessons

   c. Work on inferential comprehension through a gradual release of responsibility model

   d. Tell Fred to use contextual clues to unlock the meanings of unknown words

15. **A fifth-grade student is having difficulty with tasks requiring a search for information in a hard-copy encyclopedia. This student knows how to find the correct volume for the information she needs, and she knows how to quickly locate the entry she is looking for. Her teacher notices, however, that she reads every word in the entry even when she only needs a single item of information. Her teacher should:**

   a. Require the student to only use online information sources because the hard-copy encyclopedia format will be obsolete in the near future

   b. Teach the student to read faster by just reading nouns

   c. Teach the student to use the reading strategy of generating questions; before reading the entry, the student should decide on three questions that will be answered while reading; then the student reads selectively to only answer those questions

   d. Model and explicitly teach how to read for different purposes, especially how to scan for specific information

16. **Ms. Vanik has been using guided reading with a group of five of her students. The lessons always seem to go badly. The students in this group do not seem to understand what is going on in the stories they read. This could be because:**
    a. She should be doing guiding reading with her entire class, using an instructional aide to assist her less able readers
    b. She neglected to include a writing assignment with each guided reading lesson, for example, writing personal responses to stories in journals
    c. The five students have three different instructional reading levels
    d. She has failed to teach students how to summarize what they have read

17. **It is important that students know how to spell high-frequency words. A teacher who selects high-frequency words for a weekly spelling list could provide the following rationale for that decision:**
    a. High-frequency words, for the most part, are difficult to spell
    b. High-frequency words are those words that appear most frequently in printed English
    c. This will help children as they go about the process of mastering the most regular sound-symbol relationships in English
    d. Phonetic spellers choose at least one letter to represent each sound in words they write

18. **Mr. Kiptanui has a second-grade student who has not learned the simple sound-symbol relationships that all second graders should know. He has taught his phonics lessons following a part-to-whole approach. He should now:**
    a. Rely on language play, requiring the student to memorize two or three simple chants each week
    b. Assess his teaching, consider the alternatives, and try a whole-to-part approach
    c. Refocus on teaching the meanings of Greek and Latin root words
    d. Realize that spelling instruction in context will teach the student most of the sound-symbol relationships he needs to know

19. **A fourth-grade teacher in a small elementary school knows that both third-grade teachers do a poor job of exposing their students to expository texts. A reasonable first step toward her goal of helping her students become proficient when reading such texts is to:**
    a. Include expository texts, like biography and information books, in her read-aloud program
    b. Teach her students how to clarify meaning when they are confused
    c. Stop relying on standardized reading tests to make judgments about the reading ability of her students and start using a more comprehensive system of assessment
    d. Stress the importance of story structure through the use of story grammars, story maps, and story frames

20. **A teacher who decides to use onsets and rimes as a basis for a series of lessons for his students who are struggling with word identification could provide the following rationale for his decision:**
    a. Rimes used to be called *phonograms,* which confused students
    b. It is easy to use diagrams, charts, and illustrations to teach onsets and rimes; this will particularly help the teacher's English Learners
    c. Even though state and local content standards have inexplicably ignored onsets and rimes, standards produced by national organizations have emphasized their role in beginning reading instruction
    d. Once a student understands the graphic representation for a rime, she or he has a useful tool to decode all words that include that rime

21. **Ms. Yifter is a teacher who believes in a balanced approach to teaching reading. She understands the importance of phonemic awareness in reading development, so she teaches many directed lessons to develop her kindergarteners' acquisition of phonemic awareness. To balance these lessons she should:**
    a. Develop a series of worksheets to reinforce what the students have learned
    b. Administer a timed test to see what each student has learned
    c. Use chants and songs with rhyming words
    d. Use contextual redefinition and the clueing technique

22. **Teachers should have an assessment plan that uses a variety of measures to evaluate student development. This would include informal measures like:**
    a. Anecdotal records the teacher has carefully kept while students are engaged in reading activities
    b. A teacher-developed test of recognition of 100 high-frequency words
    c. A standardized, norm-referenced test of reading comprehension if the test includes questions assessing the following levels of comprehension: literal, inferential, and evaluative
    d. A test of concepts about print produced by the publisher of a basal reading series that includes a very specific script for the person administering the test

23. **Ms. Potenza would like her second graders to develop a sense of story structure. She thinks this will help them better understand the stories they read. She should:**
    a. Use story frames and, when students are ready, story grammars and story maps
    b. Teach her students that not all stories begin with "Once upon a time"
    c. Use guided reading lessons that focus on how different students can have different perspectives of the same event in a story
    d. Use a combination of environmental print, the shared book experience, and reading aloud

24. **It is the sixth month of school and Ms. Dombrowski is concerned. Five of her kindergarten students don't understand that the words in a story are read left to right, top to bottom. She should:**
    a. Rely on environmental print, a print-rich environment, reading aloud, and shared book experiences to teach this concept

b. Refocus her attention on phonemic awareness

c. Use a variety of instructional strategies to teach her students to use context to decode words that they do not know

d. Plan and implement direct, explicit lessons to teach directionality

25. **The English word *limousine* is derived from the French, more specifically, from the word for a hood that is part of the traditional costume of the French region of Limousin. Should a sixth-grade teacher include this information as part of a spelling lesson?**

a. No, the emphasis should be on the uniqueness of the spelling of *limousine,* especially the five vowels

b. No, lessons should be based on multisensory strategies

c. Yes, it would seem to be a good use of etymology

d. Yes, it is a good example of multicultural teaching

26. **Ms. Shuwei was a student teacher in a second-grade classroom. She told her supervisor that the next time she visited she would teach a lesson on consonant blends. Ms. Shuwei was working on *ph* as in *graph,* *ch* as in *much,* and *sh* as in *bush.* She carefully told her students that these letter combinations made a blended sound, with each letter making a sound. Her supervisor had a shocked look on her face because:**

a. She failed to include an anticipatory set in her lesson

b. These letters aren't consonant blends; they are consonant digraphs and each pair of letters makes only one sound

c. These letters aren't consonant blends; they are consonant diphthongs and each pair of letters makes a glided vowel sound

d. *Ph* as in *graph* and *ch* as in *much* should never be taught together in the same lesson

27. **Mr. Borzov wanted his third-grade students to know how to classify questions so they would be more efficient in locating answers. He agrees with the research that shows poor readers waste a great deal of time looking for the answers to questions whose answers cannot be found in one place in the text. He should:**

a. Include literal, inferential, and evaluative questions in each guided reading lesson

b. Be sure that he uses a pre-reading activity to activate background knowledge, like a KWL chart

c. Work on teaching inferential and evaluative comprehension skills and teach students the relationship between different types of questions and the locations of their answers

d. Begin each lesson with a CLOZE exercise

28. **Mr. Berruti wants his fourth graders to use context to unlock the meanings of words they do not know. He will plan activities that will help his students use semantic clues, which are:**

a. The meanings of surrounding words

b. Clues based on word order

c. Inappropriate for fourth graders because they are too easy

d. A part of morphemic analysis

29. **Sally is a fifth-grade student. She is not a fluent reader. She reads very slowly, especially when she reads in her science textbook. To help her, her teacher is teaching her the meanings of difficult words she will encounter in each chapter of the science textbook. What else could Sally's teacher do?**

   a. Improve Sally's reading self-image by giving her tangible rewards for positive behaviors

   b. Use paired reading: Have Sally read aloud with a more competent peer who will read at a rate that is slightly faster than Sally's

   c. Have Sally read more orally; she needs more practice

   d. Place Sally in a group with other readers having difficulty with the grade-level science book; then have them use a science book at the third- or fourth-grade level

30. **Ms. Rudolph teaches kindergarten. She has a group of students who are having difficulty with sound isolation and matching activities. For these students, she has decided to regularly read aloud books with wordplay, such as *Each Peach Pear Plum*. This should help her students because:**

   a. This type of book focuses on the sounds in words, and this is what phonemic awareness is all about

   b. The initial /p/ sound is highly regular, so she made a good choice with that book

   c. Phonemic awareness is a strong predictor of early reading success

   d. This type of book includes illustrations, which help children understand the sounds

31. **Ms. Vandereycken teaches third grade. Her school district has purchased a new reading program, complete with several components. She wants to meet the needs of all her students. Her students read at a wide variety of instructional levels, everything from primer to fifth grade. What should she do?**

   a. Develop a set of tests for each area of reading development; administer them to her students; use the results to create instructional groups

   b. Create three groups for reading instruction

   c. Refer her low readers for possible special education placement

   d. Use flexible grouping, individualized reading instruction, and timely intervention for those children having difficulty

32. **Benoit is a seventh-grade student. His language arts teacher has planned several literature-based units around genres. For each unit, the teacher reads aloud one book and bases many literary analysis lessons on that book (e.g., for his unit on high fantasy, he read aloud *A Wizard of Earthsea*). The teacher also brings to class a wide selection of books within the genre, so each student can read something at his or her independent reading level. Benoit is a strong reader—his instructional reading level is eighth grade. He had difficulty, however, with a science fiction novel that had a readability level of fifth grade. What should Benoit's teacher do?**

a. Teach Benoit the features of science fiction, including the characters, settings, plots, and style unique to that genre

b. Help Benoit find a science fiction novel written at a lower readability level

c. Teach Benoit how to generate questions after he has read the first paragraph of a new chapter

d. Have Benoit read a book in the *Star Wars* series because the films will make it easier for him to comprehend what he is reading

33. **Ms. Jacobs is a first-grade teacher. She has assessed her students and determined that over half of them are at the pre-phonetic level of spelling development. To help these students become more accurate spellers, she should:**

a. Start by assessing the students' mastery of common prefixes and suffixes

b. Require the children to learn three sight words each week

c. Explicitly teach children the etymology of the 20 words that appear most frequently in printed English

d. Be sure the students have phonemic awareness; if they do, proceed to assess and teach phonics

34. **Ms. Kratzenberg teaches fifth grade. In her classroom there are seven English Learners who have an instructional reading level of Grade 3 in English. During teacher-directed reading lessons, Ms. Kratzenberg should:**

a. Ask students to read aloud every day, without practice, and in random order

b. Be sure to use the comprehension questions that appear at the bottom of each page in the teachers' edition of the basal reader

c. Divide the lesson into three parts: First, teach basic literacy concepts, such as the directionality of English; second, focus on morphemic analysis, especially Greek and Latin root words; third, read through the story, stopping at the end of each paragraph to ask literal comprehension questions

d. Use a variety of strategies to support these students, including preview-review, visual aids, charts, and real objects

35. **Jerry is a sixth-grade student. When asked to read the fifth-grade passage in an Informal Reading Inventory, his word identification was 95%, but he missed 4 out of 10 comprehension questions. Jerry's teacher told him that this showed that his instructional reading level is fifth grade. This means:**

a. The teacher made a mistake; if Jerry's word identification is 95% or higher, then the text is at his independent reading level

b. Jerry's comprehension is not at an acceptable level, and the problem is not poor word identification skills

c. Jerry received too much intensive phonics instruction when he was younger

d. Jerry's frustration reading level will be at Grade 4

36. **Ms. Romero teaches third grade. She wants to do a better job of selecting spelling words for her students to learn. She should:**

a. Organize her spelling lists by grouping words by syllable length, and be sure that each week's list includes words of one, two, and three syllables

b. Find a list of the rimes that occur must frequently in printed English; then encourage her students to include words with those rimes in their journals

c. Create lists of words based on orthographic patterns and high-frequency words that do not conform to those patterns

d. Realize that no systematic approach to teaching spelling works; some children will always have difficulty with spelling

37. **Mr. Kail is a second-grade teacher. He wants all of his students to spend at least 30 minutes a day reading independently. He knows that this will not be an issue for some of his students, but that independent reading will be an area of need for many others. He individually administered a Reading Interest Survey; each student responded orally to the questions. What other data will provide him with information about the independent reading habits of his students?**

a. The responses students write in their journals, after he has read aloud

b. Each student's independent reading level, as determined by an informal reading inventory

c. The results of a simple assessment of each student's letter recognition and phonemic awareness

d. His observations of student behavior during Sustained Silent Reading time

38. **Mr. Nguyen is concerned about the difficulty many of his students have reading their fourth-grade social studies textbooks. He should:**

a. Thoroughly assess the phonemic awareness of each student having difficulty

b. Teach a series of lessons on how to use the structure of expository text to improve comprehension

c. Teach several word identification strategies including phonics, sight words, and morphemic analysis

d. Realize the importance of narrative text structures and use those structures to help improve comprehension

39. **Ms. Chin is a second-grade teacher. Within the same week, two new students from Italy joined her classroom. Paolo just moved to the United States from Naples. Paolo is a good reader and writer in Italian, but he does not speak any English. Angelina was born in Rome. Angelina's parents have moved several times; she has lived in Paris, Buenos Aires, and New York. As a result, she cannot read or write in Italian. She, too, does not speak English. Which of the following is a reasonable option for Ms. Chin?**

a. Paolo will not need to be taught most of the English concepts about print; Angelina will need this instruction

b. Paolo knows how to read; he can be placed in a group reading a grade-level text

c. Angelina will not need any English phonemic awareness lessons because Italian is a Latin-based language

d. Before beginning any English reading instruction, each student must be able to speak at least 100 English words

40. **Mr. Jackson's second-grade students draw as a pre-writing activity. Although he believes this is a good way for young writers to organize their thoughts, he wants to expand their repertoire of pre-writing tools, so he could introduce:**
    a. A test of phonemic awareness, like the Yopp-Singer Test of Phonemic Segmentation
    b. Lessons on proofreading; beginning with how to find errors of capitalization; then errors of punctuation; finally, errors of usage
    c. Developmentally appropriate pre-writing strategies that use the features of literary genres as organizing frameworks for creative writing assignments
    d. A developmentally appropriate technique, like Quick Write

41. **Fred, a third-grade student, has completed a standardized, norm-referenced test of reading comprehension. He correctly answered 40 of the 50 questions on this exam. Which of the following would be a reasonable set of scores for Fred?**
    a. A percentile score of 88 and a grade-level equivalent score of 5.7
    b. A percentile score of 88 and a grade-level equivalent score of 1.7
    c. A percentile score of 28 and a grade-level equivalent score of 5.7
    d. A percentile score of 28 and a grade-level equivalent score of 1.7

42. **On the graded reading passages of an Informal Reading Inventory (IRI), a student's independent, instructional, and frustration reading levels are determined by:**
    a. Knowledge of sound-symbol relationships and performance on a spelling test
    b. Percentage of oral reading miscues and percentage of correct answers to comprehension questions
    c. Percentage of oral reading miscues and rate of reading
    d. Number of words skipped divided by the number of words repeated

43. **Ms. Harris teaches fourth grade. She is teaching a series of lessons on the use of simile and metaphor in children's literature. This will help students better understand an author's use of:**
    a. The author's adaptation of text structures that compare and contrast
    b. Mood and tone—the ambience of the story
    c. Figurative language
    d. Integral setting

44. **Mr. Redab is a third-grade teacher. Last year, he didn't do a very good job of teaching reading. Almost all of his lessons were on phonics, sight words, and structural analysis. Mr. Redab's principal told him that, among other things, his instructional program was not comprehensive. Mr. Redab thought his program was comprehensive. After all, he was teaching his students three different word identification strategies. Mr. Redab needs to understand that a comprehensive instructional program in reading is one that:**
    a. Utilizes all the components of the reading series the district has adopted, not just the teacher's edition and the students' texts
    b. Also includes instruction in several other areas, like comprehension

c. Places vocabulary teaching at the center, with appropriate time for word identification and comprehension instruction

d. Balances two sets of standards, those approved by the district and those approved by the state of California

45. **Ms. Davis, a second-grade teacher, wants her students to read independently at home. She asked her students to complete a chart, logging the minutes they read at home every day for a week. She was worried that several of her students never seem to read at home. Almost all of her students are Spanish-speaking English Learners. To support at-home reading, she should:**

a. Send a letter to the home of each student, written in Spanish and English, informing parents of their responsibility to help their children succeed in school

b. Contact the librarian in the children's literature department of the local public library; find out about the library's collection of children's books written in Spanish

c. Create an individualized reading plan for each of her students, providing a list of 25 books that should be read independently sometime during the school year

d. Focus her energy on the effective teaching of word identification and comprehension

46. **Mr. Ramirez teaches sixth grade. He wants to determine who among his students will have difficulty with the sixth-grade science book. He should:**

a. Develop and administer tests of student knowledge of the etymology and morphology of specific "science" words

b. Use the following sources of information: the results of a standardized, norm-referenced reading comprehension test administered the year before; the results of an IRI; the results of a CLOZE test from the science textbook

c. Use the following sources of information: the results of a standardized, norm-referenced reading comprehension test administered the year before; the results of an IRI; the results of a test of word identification strategies

d. Randomly select 50 words from two pages in the middle of the science text, then ask each student to read the words aloud

47. **Children in the precommunicative stage of spelling development:**

a. Should have a program of reading instruction that focuses on learning sight words, especially the 50 words that appear most frequently in printed English

b. Will, for the most part, not want to take part in playful language activities, like chanting and singing

c. Do not use graphophonemic relationships when they write

d. Should have a program of reading instruction that focuses on phonics

48. **A group of fifth-grade students is having difficulty using commas appropriately in their writing. They use commas correctly with items in a series**

(e.g., *salmon, tuna, and cod are all fish*) and when they write the date. Other than that, they rarely use a comma correctly. Their teacher should:

    a. Develop and implement a series of teacher-directed lessons to teach the proper use of commas

    b. Avoid calling attention to these errors so students maintain positive self-images as writers

    c. Place the errors in context; as long as their written messages are comprehensible there is no need for concern

    d. Develop and implement a series of teacher-directed lessons to teach the proper use of capital letters

49. **A first-grade teacher who wants to assess the reading comprehension of her students may decide to have her students retell a story they have read. This form of assessment will, in most cases, assess which of the following?**

    a. Literal comprehension of the story

    b. Knowledge of high-frequency words

    c. Inferential comprehension of the story

    d. Knowledge of sound-symbol relationships

50. **Once a teacher determines a child's level of spelling development, she or he should:**

    a. Find the relationship between that level and the child's instructional reading level

    b. Work with the child to make sure the child does not overemphasize correctness

    c. Attempt to help the child "move through" that level and on to the next

    d. Rely on the lists of words provided by the spelling book

51. **Ms. Koolagonta wants to improve the reading comprehension of her students. She has assessed their different strengths and weaknesses. She has determined that six of her third graders do a good job remembering the sequence and details of the stories they read, but they have difficulty when asked to summarize the main themes of these same stories. She should:**

    a. Develop and implement a series of lessons that focus on the contextual clues that unlock the meanings of unknown words

    b. Conduct further assessment of this group of students to determine whether they are better at remembering story sequence or detail

    c. Use multisensory teaching techniques, including kinesthetic and tactile approaches, to teach summarization

    d. Begin by modeling the process of identifying possible themes and restating them in simple sentences

52. **A first-grade teacher who wants her students to know where to find the name of a book's author and title should:**

    a. Realize that many resources can be used to teach these concepts about print, including the Language Experience Approach and environmental print

    b. Assess each student, and then use student names as a basis for teaching these concepts

c. Assess each student, and then teach these concepts directly

d. Always point out the author and title when doing a shared book experience

53. **A test of phonemic awareness could ask students to perform any of the following tasks: sound matching, sound isolation, sound blending, sound addition and substitution, and sound segmentation. Why might a teacher want to start with a test of sound segmentation?**
    a. A test of sound segmentation is easy to develop
    b. This is the easiest of the phonemic awareness tasks
    c. This is the most difficult of the phonemic awareness tasks
    d. Because starting with sound matching requires the use of words with three and four syllables

54. **After reading *Ella Enchanted,* a fifth-grade boy writes in his journal: "This was a pretty good story. My sister, Asha, is smart and she is clumsy, just like Ella." This is an example of a student:**
    a. Not understanding what he has read
    b. Analyzing the text using the literary elements
    c. Making a personal connection with literature
    d. Using genre as a basis for organizing a response

55. **Rontrey is a fourth-grade student who rarely says anything during the meetings of his literature study group. Rontrey is a strong reader with above-grade-level skills in comprehension and vocabulary. In one-on-one conversations, he is highly verbal. What could his teacher do to encourage him to say more during discussions?**
    a. Explain to Rontrey that his grade in reading depends on him speaking up more
    b. Conduct an individual conference with Rontrey before the group meets to give him a chance to practice
    c. Place Rontrey in a different group
    d. Have Rontrey memorize three comments before each group meeting

56. **Ms. Petrymyas has decided to use a semantic map to teach her children the meanings of three words they will encounter during a reading assignment in their social studies textbook. During the lesson, the students will:**
    a. Learn the difference between derivational and inflectional suffixes
    b. Look at a list of attributes for the three words and then decide whether each attribute fits each word
    c. Write each word in some sort of personal dictionary
    d. Use diagrams to organize words and phrases that define each word

57. **When reading expository text, students frequently will read "differently" than when they read a narrative text. They might, for example, have to skim or scan. This most likely would occur when a student:**
    a. Reads to locate information in an encyclopedia
    b. Reads a chapter in a social studies textbook

c. Reads a biography of Olympic athlete Marion Jones

d. Reads a poem written about track star Michael Johnson

58. **Mr. Hana-Rigelman has used graphic organizers to provide students a preview of what they will be asked to read in social studies textbooks. The organizers don't seem to be working. This could be because:**

a. Each organizer consists of only three to five words

b. He has used the structure of the text to develop graphic organizers

c. He presents the graphic organizers to his students before they read

d. Each organizer is a chart summarizing what content the children learn when they read

59. **Ms. Kipkeni has five fifth-grade students whose instructional reading level is fourth grade. She is determined that each of these students will meet her state's English Language Arts Content Standards for Grade 5. She has:**

a. Made a significant teaching error; the standards were never meant for every student

b. A poor understanding of the role standards are supposed to play; they were never meant to be the basis for how instruction is designed

c. A good understanding of the role standards play; they were meant for every student

d. Made a significant teaching error; the teachers' edition of the reading textbook series she uses will define what students should know and be able to do

60. **Many teachers use onsets and rimes to improve the word identification skills of their students. This is because:**

a. It makes sense to teach onsets and rimes because most young children are not ready to recognize the number of phonemes in a word

b. Once children know the definitions of *onset* and *rime*, they can determine which syllables have an onset and a rime and which have only a rime

c. Of all the word identification strategies children use, phonics is the least effective

d. The most common rimes appear repeatedly in English words

61. **Ms. Wang wants her seventh-grade students to know how to use morphemic clues to unlock the meanings of words they do not know. She should teach:**

a. The importance of reading every word in a text

b. The meanings of Greek- and Latin-based root words

c. How to increase reading fluency

d. How to divide words into syllables

62. **Which of the following best describes a characteristic of effective phonics instruction?**

a. It is child-centered: The instruction relies primarily on teaching sound-symbol relationships that children are most interested in learning

b. It is embedded: Most phonics instruction takes place as part of other language experiences

c. It is systematic: Instruction is sequenced according to the increased complexity of linguistic units

d. It is equitable: So that no child feels separated, all children should take part in each phonics lesson

63. **Ms. Tran, a fourth-grade teacher, decides to develop her own reading comprehension test. Students will read a selection from an old fourth-grade basal reader. She has written nine questions. Three of the questions assess literal comprehension, three assess inferential comprehension, and three assess evaluative comprehension. She shows the test to the reading specialist working at her school, who responds that the test lacks validity. This could be because the test Ms. Tran created:**

a. Included questions at all three levels of comprehension

b. Has fewer than 10 questions; valid tests have at least 10

c. Had an answer key that showed the single correct answer for each question

d. Required students to write in cursive

64. **Normandy is a third-grade student. At the beginning of the year, her teacher gives her a quick test of her ability to identify words. Normandy has a very difficult time, missing 4 of 10 words on the primer list, 7 of 10 on the first-grade list, and all 10 on the second-grade list. Normandy's teacher immediately calls her parents and informs them that he is very concerned about Normandy's reading. The teacher should also:**

a. Inquire, in a diplomatic fashion, if either parent experienced difficulty in learning to read

b. Provide the parents with a list of "Ten Things Parents Can Do to Help Their Child Learn to Read"

c. Tell Normandy's parents that he will need to learn more about Normandy's strengths and needs by reviewing her cumulative record and conducting other assessments

d. Arrange a time when they can all sit down together and talk

65. **Ms. Bazile is the principal of E. B. White Elementary School. She visited a second-grade classroom and met with the teacher after school. Ms. Bazile told the teacher, "I was so impressed with how you have organized your classroom library. You really have made it easy for students to find books that they are able to read." The teacher might have:**

a. Restricted access to the classroom library so that students only go there when the teacher or an instructional aide can assist them in selecting a book

b. Prepared a bulletin board next to the classroom library featuring the last 10 winners of the Caldecott Medal

c. Chosen only 50 books for the library; for each book she has highlighted in yellow the words that last year's students could not identify

d. Organized the books by independent reading level

66. **At the beginning of the school year, teachers should complete an IRI for each of their students. The IRI will include graded reading passages; students will read aloud several of these passages. The teacher will complete a miscue analysis of these oral reading episodes. Why?**
   a. Students enjoy reading aloud; there are many tests in an IRI, and it is important that the testing process include some activities the children find enjoyable
   b. All California children are required to take reading tests in the spring of each year; these tests all include oral reading
   c. The miscue analysis will reveal which children are able to answer evaluative comprehension questions
   d. The analysis provides information needed to determine each child's instructional reading level

67. **Mr. Assiz is a kindergarten teacher. He wants his students to develop an understanding of word boundaries, which is knowing:**
   a. The number of letters in a word
   b. The configuration of words (i.e., their "shape")
   c. Where one word ends and another begins
   d. The first and last sound of a word

68. **A fourth-grade student reads aloud at a pace that is too fast. Further, he fails to pause at appropriate places in the text. His teacher should:**
   a. Model reading at an appropriate pace and with appropriate pauses; then have the student practice in individual sessions
   b. Teach the student the meaning of words with three and four syllables
   c. Always ask the student to retell what he has read
   d. Be thankful—the real problem is when students read too slowly

69. **"Strategic" readers choose to implement a variety of interventions when they are reading. These include:**
   a. The ability to distinguish characters from setting
   b. Use of the library to find specific details
   c. The use of phonemic awareness to segment words
   d. Stopping to clarify, perhaps by re-reading a paragraph

70. **Mr. Smith is a fifth-grade teacher. He has tested a student and learned that this student has very poor word identification skills. In fact, the student struggles with consonant blends, consonant digraphs, and diphthongs. Mr. Smith should:**
   a. Teach this student those sound-symbol relationships
   b. Focus on fifth-grade word identification tasks, like learning the meanings of common Greek and Latin root words
   c. Place the student in a second-grade classroom during reading time
   d. Work on skimming and scanning, important content-area reading skills for fifth grade

ESSAY QUESTIONS

Number One

Answer the following in approximately 50 words. Use the information below to write your answer.

Mr. Lopez is a first-grade teacher. He has 19 students. Mr. Lopez wants to administer an informal reading inventory to each of his students. The IRI will include graded word lists and graded word passages. He is not sure what other types of tests to include.

(1) Using your knowledge of reading assessment, write a response in which you describe one other type of test Mr. Lopez should include in his IRIs.

Number Two

Answer the following in approximately 50 words. Use the information below to write your answer.

Ms. MacDowell teaches fourth grade. She has six students who are English Learners. Four are native Spanish speakers and two are native Cantonese speakers. All have made good progress in acquiring oral English. The results of an IRI in English showed that three of the students have an instructional reading level of Grade 3; and three of the ELs have a much lower instructional reading level, Grade 1.

(2) Write a response that describes how Ms. MacDowell should organize reading instruction for these six students.

Number Three

Answer the following in approximately 150 words. Use the information below to write your answer.

Ms. Tamas is a sixth-grade teacher. She has four students whose instructional reading level is Grade 5. This group of students shares a common reading preference: They all like reading comic books. These students do okay when they read from their sixth-grade basal readers, but they are having difficulty with their social studies and science textbooks.

(3) Write a response in which you (a) describe an instructional strategy or activity that Ms. Tamas can implement to help these students better understand their social studies and science textbooks, and (b) explain why the strategy or activity you describe would be effective.

Number Four

Answer the following in approximately 150 words. Use the information below to write your answer.

Ms. Oglesby's first-grade class includes a student, Peyton, who is having a great deal of difficulty with reading tasks. A look at Peyton's cumulative record reveals that he missed 65 school days in kindergarten due to injuries he suffered in an automobile accident (he is fine now). He thought there were three sounds in the words *at, boo,* and *elephant.* Peyton could not identify rhyming pairs of words. He could not identify the author and the title of a book Ms. Oglesby read to him. When Ms. Oglesby asked Peyton to help her read the book, he seemed to have no idea what to do when he came to the end of a line.

(4) Write a response in which you (a) identify one area of need demonstrated by Peyton, (b) describe an instructional strategy or activity to help address this need, and (c) explain why the strategy or activity you describe would be effective for this purpose.

Number Five: Case Study

This case study focuses on Julie, who is seven years old and in the second grade. Her primary language is English. Her health is fine; her vision and hearing have been tested and are normal. She tries her best in school. The documents on the following pages describe Julie's reading performance during the middle of the school year (in January, traditional calendar). Using these materials, write a response in which you apply your knowledge of reading assessment and instruction. Your response should include three parts:

1. Identify three of Julie's reading strengths and/or needs at this point in the school year, citing evidence from the documents to support your conclusions;
2. Describe two specific instructional strategies and/or activities designed to foster Julie's literacy development for the remainder of the school year by addressing the needs and/or building on the strengths you identified; and
3. Explain how each strategy/activity you describe would promote Julie's reading proficiency.

Test of Letter Recognition

The 26 letters of the alphabet were arranged randomly. Julie was asked to read them. She read all the letters correctly. Score: 26/26.

Informal Reading Assessment

Printed below is the record Julie's teacher made of her oral reading. Julie was asked to read the selection aloud. As Julie read, the teacher kept a record of her performance.

This is a first-grade passage from the *Bader Reading and Language Inventory* (3rd ed.).

Pat and the Kitten

Pat saw a kitten. It was on the ‖ ^T side of the ‖ ^T street. It was ‖ ^T sitting under a blue car.

"Come here, little kitten," Pat said. The kitten looked (up at) ^LIKED Pat. It had big yellow

eyes. Pat took her from under the car. She saw that her leg was hurt. ^HIT

"I will take care of you." Pat said. She put her hand on the kitten's ‖ ^T soft, black fur.

"You can come home with me."

The kitten gave a happy *meow*.

Teacher's notes: 80 words, 7 errors. Julie does not pause when she sees a comma and she does not stop when she comes to the end of a sentence. She reads as if the punctuation were not there.

Key: ○ deletion | short pause   ← repetition

© self-correction   ‖ long pause   ^CAT⁄COW substitution

T teacher provided the word after a long pause

Julie's teacher let Julie read the selection silently. Then she asked Julie to retell the story. Below is a record of the items she mentioned during this unaided recall.

___✓___ Pat saw a kitten
___✓___ on the side of a street/under a car
_____ come here, Pat said
_____ kitten looked up
___✓___ big yellow eyes, black fur
_____ her leg was hurt
___✓___ I will take care of you
_____ Pat put hand on fur
___✓___ come home with me
___✓___ kitten meowed happily
Score: 6/10

Results of Phonics Tests

Julie was asked to read lists of words.

Initial consonants	9/10	(missed word with initial *s*)
Initial blends	8/10	(missed *st* in *stay* and *spr* in *spring*)
Digraphs	6/10	(missed words starting with *ph*, *ch*)
Ending sounds	8/10	(didn't say *s* in *plants,* read *bet* for *beach*)
Medial vowels	8/10	(read *met* for *meet* and *did* for *dead*)

Test of Basic Sight Words

In a test of 50 basic sight words (selected randomly from Fry's 240 "Instant Words"), Julie correctly identified 42 of the 50 words. She missed: *know, because, again, away, thought, beginning, together, took.*

Interest Inventory

The teacher read the questions. Julie gave her answers orally:

Think of all the things we do in our classroom. Think about everything from when we get here in the morning until we leave at night. What do you like best? *Mmmmm, that's hard. I like when we go outside and play games. I also like to act in plays.*

Do you have a favorite book? *Yes. It's the book you read to us yesterday about the grandfather from Japan. He went back to Japan.*

If you could do anything you wanted for one hour, what would it be? *That's easy. I would play soccer and then go swimming.*

Do you have a favorite movie? *Yes. I like* The Little Mermaid. *My grandma gave it to me last year for my birthday.*

Do you read at home? *A little, when I don't have anything else to do. Well, actually my big sister who is in the other school likes to read to me. But not as much as she used to. My mom and dad watch television more.*

Answers to the Sample Examination

MULTIPLE CHOICE*

1. A   Reading aloud will provide children with an understanding of story structure. If you missed this question, you should take another look at Chapter 3.

2. C   Shared book experiences require the use of a big book. HELP: Chapter 3.

3. A   If the teacher selects the topics for LEA sessions, then many children will have little, if anything, to say. Children should select most of the topics to stimulate their dictation. HELP: Chapter 3.

4. B   Big books are not environmental print. Environmental print includes those texts that are not produced for educational purposes. HELP: Chapter 4.

5. A   None of the other choices make sense. There are several things Mr. Ribiero could do, and teaching meaning vocabulary is one of them. HELP: Chapter 9.

6. D   Punctuation requires pauses and stops. To understand most texts, the reader must understand the role punctuation marks play. HELP: Chapter 8 and Chapter 14.

7. A   Meaning vocabulary lessons work best if the target words are related to each other. The relationship can be orthographic (e.g., words all with the rime *ight*) or topical. Words that are essential to understanding a story also are good choices for vocabulary lessons. HELP: Chapter 9.

8. D   If first graders routinely have difficulty with sounds at the end of words, it is a good idea to do a phonemic awareness test to be sure they are aware of those sounds. HELP: Chapter 5.

9. B   If ELs have learned to read in the first language, then there will be both positive and negative transfer to the challenge of reading in English. Latin-based languages, like Spanish, are read left to right, top to bottom, like English. This English concept of print need not be taught to students who can read Spanish. HELP: Chapter 9.

10. C   Thorough assessment is the first step to improving phonics instruction at this hypothetical school. HELP: Chapter 5.

11. A   This was a sound identity task, a part of acquiring phonemic awareness. HELP: Chapter 4.

12. C   This is an issue of balance. In addition to the direct, explicit vocabulary teaching Ms. Keino will do, she must balance that instruction with a plan to increase the independent reading of her students. HELP: Chapter 12.

*After each explanation, I indicate the relevant chapter.

13. B   To connect children to appropriate books, the teacher would need to know the independent reading levels of her students. HELP: Chapter 12.

14. A   Fred needs tools to figure out the meanings of words he does not know. Structural or morphemic analysis, including lessons on the meanings of prefixes and suffixes, is one way to do this. Answer (d) is incorrect because Mr. Serdula will need to do more than just tell Fred to use contextual clues. Fred will have to be taught how to use them. HELP: Chapter 9.

15. D   This student needs to know how to read quickly until she finds what she is looking for. HELP: Chapter 10.

16. C   Guided reading lessons require that students be grouped by their instructional reading levels. HELP: Chapter 8.

17. B   Because they appear so often in printed English, high-frequency words are a good choice for inclusion on a spelling list. HELP: Chapter 7.

18. B   If one approach to teaching phonics directly and explicitly doesn't work, the teacher should try another. HELP: Chapter 5.

19. A   A teacher who wants to introduce her students to expository texts should select information books, biographies, and encyclopedia entries to read to her students. HELP: Chapter 10.

20. D   Rimes are a good thing to know because common rimes appear in many English words (like the *at* in *bat, cat, rat,* etc.). HELP: Chapter 5.

21. C   Again, this is a question of balance. These direct, explicit lessons should be balanced with lighthearted activities with rhyming words, like chants and songs. HELP: Chapter 1.

22. A   The other options are formal assessments. HELP: Chapter 2.

23. A   Story frames, story grammars, and story maps are all devices teachers use to teach story structure. HELP: Chapter 8.

24. D   At this point, direct intervention is necessary. HELP: Chapter 3.

25. C   This would be a perfect time to focus on etymology, because the spelling of *limousine* so closely parallels *Limousin.* If the use of etymology were not so obvious, then (b) would be correct. HELP: Chapter 7.

26. B   The supervisor was shocked because Ms. Shuwei didn't know the difference between consonant blends and consonant digraphs. HELP: Chapter 5.

27. C   Students can be taught the differences among literal, inferential, and evaluative questions and how to answer each type of question. HELP: Chapter 8.

28. A   Semantics refers to word meaning. HELP: Chapter 9.

29. B   Paired reading is an accepted approach to improving fluency. D is not a correct answer because science textbooks at other grade levels won't fit the fifth-grade science standards. HELP: Chapter 6.

30. A Alliteration helps students acquire phonemic awareness. HELP: Chapter 4.

31. D In almost any classroom there will be children with widely different reading abilities. From an organizational standpoint, to meet the needs of diverse students, teachers must use flexible grouping, individualized instruction, and intervention with children having particular difficulty. HELP: Chapter 1.

32. A One way to improve students' comprehension of any genre is to teach them the features of that genre. HELP: Chapter 11.

33. D Pre-phonetic spellers do not assign at least one letter to each sound in a word. The first step is to determine if they recognize all the sounds in words. HELP: Chapter 7.

34. D This menu of strategies can provide the "scaffolding" necessary in a reading lesson with English Learners. HELP: Chapter 15.

35. B The high threshold for word identification (90%) at the instructional level means that the comprehension problems are not the result of poor word identification skills. HELP: Chapter 2.

36. C Spelling lists should include both words that follow the orthographic patterns of English (like *date, hope, time*) and those "outlaw" words that do not (*love*). HELP: Chapter 7.

37. D Observation of student behavior during Sustained Silent Reading time will reveal information about how each student behaves when asked to read independently. HELP: Chapter 12.

38. B Text structure, like compare and contrast, can be used to prepare graphic organizers and study guides. HELP: Chapter 10.

39. A Many concepts about print transfer from Italian to English. Paolo doesn't need to be retaught those concepts. Angelina is starting from scratch. HELP: Chapter 15.

40. D Quick Write is a simple pre-writing activity. HELP: Chapter 13.

41. A It is impossible to determine precisely which percentile and grade-level equivalent scores would be assigned to Fred. It would all depend on the previous performance of the sampling group. A percentile score of 88 and grade-level equivalent score of 5.7 seem about right. HELP: Chapter 2.

42. B Two factors determine reading levels on an IRI: number of miscues and number of questions answered correctly. HELP: Chapter 2.

43. C Simile and metaphor are examples of figurative language. HELP: Chapter 11.

44. B Comprehensive instruction covers all of the RICA content areas, not just one. HELP: Chapter 1.

45. B At-home reading can be in any language and should include parent participation. Informing parents of first-language resources is essential. (A) is not correct because almost all parents are aware of their responsibility to help their children.

Rather than lecture parents, a letter from a teacher should propose ways for parents to work with the teacher and with their children. HELP: Chapter 12.

46. B   It is important to include the use of a CLOZE test because it is text-specific. HELP: Chapter 10.

47. C   Precommunicative spellers use symbols other than letters, and their choice of letters is random in that the letters do not represent sounds. HELP: Chapter 7.

48. A   It is time to teach this group of students how to use commas. HELP: Chapter 14.

49. A   Retellings assess literal comprehension. HELP: Chapter 8.

50. C   The goal of spelling development is to help children progress through the stage they are in and move on to the next stage. HELP: Chapter 7.

51. D   The best way to begin to teach summarizing is for the teacher to model it through "think-alouds." HELP: Chapter 8.

52. C   First assess, then teach to those who have not acquired this concept about print. HELP: Chapter 3.

53. C   If a child can segment words, that is, identify how many sounds are in a word and name those sounds, then the chances are that she can complete the other, simpler phonemic awareness tasks. HELP: Chapter 4.

54. C   Recognizing a link between a living person and a fictional character shows the student has made a personal connection with the book. HELP: Chapter 11.

55. B   This seems to be the best choice—give the student a chance to practice. HELP: Chapter 13.

56. D   Semantic maps are diagrams. HELP: Chapter 9.

57. A   When reading an encyclopedia, efficient readers skim and scan. HELP: Chapter 10.

58. A   Graphic organizers will, in almost every case, require more than three to five words. HELP: Chapter 10.

59. C   All students are expected to achieve California's grade-level standards. HELP: Chapter 1.

60. D   The most common rimes do appear frequently in English words. HELP: Chapter 5.

61. B   Morphemic analysis uses prefixes, root words, suffixes, and compound words. HELP: Chapter 9.

62. C   Phonics instruction should be systematic in that instruction progresses from the simple sound-symbol relationships to the more complex. HELP: Chapter 5.

63. C   It is possible to create valid measures of all three levels of comprehension. There will, however, be several correct answers to inferential and evaluative questions. HELP: Chapter 8.

64. C   This is a close call, but (c) is more correct. The teacher will need to have a conference with Normandy's parents, but it will be more productive if it is conducted after he has gathered more information. HELP: Chapter 2.

65. D A library organized by independent reading levels will help students find books they are able to read. HELP: Chapter 11.

66. D A miscue analysis of oral reading must be performed to find independent, instructional, and frustration reading levels. HELP: Chapter 2.

67. C Word boundaries show where words start and finish. HELP: Chapter 3.

68. A To help this student, the teacher needs to model appropriate reading paces and monitor the student's progress in individual sessions. HELP: Chapter 6.

69. D Strategic readers know when they are confused. They stop and do something to clarify the text's meaning. HELP: Chapter 8.

70. A This fifth grader must learn these basic sound-symbol relationships. HELP: Chapter 5.

How Well Did You Do on the Multiple Choice Section?

Different state exams will have different minimum passing scores. If you answered less than 52 of the 70 questions correctly (about 75%), you should be concerned. Please note, though, that some of my questions may be easier than the ones you will answer, and some may be more difficult.

ESSAYS

Question One—Sample Answer

Mr. Lopez should select a test of phonemic awareness, such as the Yopp-Singer Test of Phonemic Segmentation. In this test, the teacher says 22 words, each with three sounds. The child must then tell the teacher each sound in the word in order. Students who do well on the test are phonemically aware. For those who do poorly, the teacher will need to assess their ability to isolate, match, substitute, and blend sounds.

Assessing Your Answer. Assessing your own essay answers will be difficult. I suggest you exchange papers with two other students who are in the teaching credential program with you. For sample essay question one, a complete answer would have described one assessment of any of the following: concepts about print, phonemic awareness, phonics, sight words. The one assessment you selected should be described in two or three sentences.

Question Two—Sample Answer

Because the students have instructional reading levels two grades apart, Ms. MacDowell should divide the students into two groups for guided reading lessons. She should use flexible grouping to teach the students the reading skills they need (like knowledge of sight words). It is possible that some groups will include children from both groups. Finally, she should provide individualized instruction to any child who is having particular difficulty.

Assessing Your Answer. The key is that children who have instructional reading levels this far apart must be separated into two groups for many activities, especially guided reading lessons that attempt to teach comprehension skills. You should also mention flexible, needs-based groups and the need for timely, individualized intervention with those children who are struggling.

Question Three—Sample Answer

Description of an Instructional Strategy or Activity. *Ms. Tamas should use expository text structures to help this group of students improve their comprehension of content-area texts. She can use the structure of chapters in the social studies text to create graphic organizers of the chapters students will read. Each graphic organizer will be a diagram with a few words. The graphic organizers will be displayed and discussed before the students start reading. Each will provide a preview of the chapter's important ideas.*

Explanation of Why the Strategy or Activity Would Be Effective. *Expository texts, like social studies and science textbooks, are written differently from narrative texts. Graphic organizers based on the structure of an expository text will show the students how each chapter is organized. The graphic organizers will provide students with a "map" they can follow as they read.*

Assessing Your Answer. The teacher could use many possible instructional interventions. You could have described activities that focus students on essential information while they read (data retrieval charts, study guides). You could have described ways for Ms. Tamas to link what the students were about to read to what they had read previously. Finally, you could have written about teaching vocabulary lessons focusing on the difficult words the students will read in their social studies or science textbooks.

Question Four—Sample Answer

Identification of One Area of Need. *Perhaps because he missed so many days of kindergarten, Peyton has not acquired some of the concepts about print he needs to become a reader. He was unable to identify authors and titles on book covers and does not understand the directionality of English.*

Description of One Instructional Strategy or Activity. *Ms. Oglesby needs to teach Peyton the concepts he lacks directly and explicitly. To teach book orientation, she will plan individualized instruction. Ms. Oglesby can use picture books she has read to the class. With Peyton, she will point out the author and title on the cover of each book, then Peyton will point to them and say the words "author" and "title." Eventually, she will challenge Peyton to make these identifications on his own while under her guidance.*

Explanation of Why the Strategy or Activity Will Be Effective. *Peyton needs direct, individualized instruction. While it is possible that Peyton will acquire some concepts about print through activities like shared book experiences, this cannot be left to chance. Direct instruction will focus on the concepts he lacks, like book orientation.*

Unless there are other children who share his needs, the lessons must be individually tailored.

Assessing Your Answer   No wiggle room here. The two areas Peyton needs to work on are concepts about print and phonemic awareness. While he undoubtedly lacks phonics skills and knowledge of many high-frequency words, the question doesn't mention either area. Only give yourself three points if you identified either concepts about print and phonemic awareness, described one way to teach to that need, and offered a good explanation.

QUESTION FIVE: CASE STUDY

Sample Answer

Three Strengths/Needs

Need: Fluency, Role of Punctuation Marks. The teacher's notes after the Informal Reading Assessment reveal Julie doesn't pause when she sees a comma and she doesn't stop at the end of sentences.

Need: Word Identification, Phonics. The results of the Phonics Tests show Julie needs to complete her knowledge of sound-symbol relationships. The results of the Informal Reading Assessment show she has problems with *s* sounds. She could not identify *side, sitting,* and *soft.* She also needs to master digraphs. She had trouble with the consonant digraphs *ph* and *ch*, and she missed two-vowel combinations in the words *meet* and *dead.*

Need: Independent Reading. Julie would benefit greatly if she increased the amount of time she reads on her own. The Interest Inventory showed she likes to play outside (soccer, swimming) and that she only reads when she has "nothing else to do."

Two Instructional Strategies/Activities

Reader's Theater for Fluency/Punctuation. In the Interest Inventory, Julie said, "I also like to act in plays." Julie's teacher should include Julie in several reader's theater productions. She reads well enough to be successful in presentations based on simple picture books. During rehearsals, Julie's teacher should model pausing when the text has a comma and stopping when she comes to the end of a sentence.

Direct Phonics Lessons for Word Identification. Julie needs direct, explicit phonics instruction. A good place to start would be with *s* in the initial position. Given the number of words Julie does know, it might be best for her teacher to start with lessons following a whole-to-part (analytic) format. The first lesson could display three of the words she didn't know in sentences (*side, sitting, soft*). After each sentence is read, the target words are circled and the target sound is emphasized.

How Each Strategy/Activity Will Help

Reader's Theater. Reader's theater requires repeated readings of the same text, usually after a model provided by the teacher. Repeated readings will teach Julie to read at an appropriate pace, with appropriate pauses and stops, and with proper inflection. Julie likes dramatic activities, so she should do well.

Direct Phonics Lessons. Children who have not acquired the sound-symbol relationships appropriate for their grade level need to be taught them directly. The type of lessons described previously is based on a thorough assessment of her specific needs. The whole-to-part format would seem best for a student who already knows many words.

Assessing Your Answer

Strengths and Weaknesses. In addition to what I mentioned, you could have written about Julie's sight vocabulary. It is both a strength in that she correctly identified 42 of the 50 words, and a weakness in that she missed some fairly easy words. Her retelling was relatively good, but I don't think there is enough there to classify her comprehension abilities. Please be sure that you cited specific evidence from the case study in this part of your answer.

Instructional Strategies/Explanation. There really are dozens of possibilities here. You could have written about ways to improve her sight vocabulary. You could have addressed ways to increase her independent reading. Another choice would have been a description of the direct teaching of end punctuation marks.

Assess your answer for clarity. Was each part of your answer clearly labeled? The question only asked for three strengths/weaknesses. You should not have identified more than three. Did you explain why your instructional strategies would work?

FINAL WORDS

Elementary school teaching is a wonderful career, full of stimulating challenges and priceless rewards. I hope you go on to be a successful teacher. Good luck!

For Further Reading

The content in this book comes from four types of sources, which should be used by anyone who wants to know more about how to teach children to read:

Major Reviews of the Research on Reading Instruction

A variety of factors have led to the publication in recent years of comprehensive reviews of the research on reading instruction. For example:

Farstrup, A. E., & Samuels, S. J. (eds.). (2002). *What research has to say about reading instruction.* Newark, DE: International Reading Association.

Kamil, M. L., Mosenthal, P. B., Pearson, P. D., & Barr, R. (eds.). (2000). *Handbook of reading research (Vol. III).* Mahwah, NJ: Lawrence Erlbaum.

National Institute of Child Health and Development (2000). *Report of the National Reading Panel. Teaching children to read: An evidence-based assessment of the scientific research literature on reading and its implication for reading instruction. Reports of the subgroups.* Washington, DC: National Institute of Child Health and Human Development/U.S. Department of Education/National Institute for Literacy. U.S. Government Printing Office, NIH Publication No. 00-04-04789.

Snow, C. E., Burns, M. S., & Griffin, P. (eds.). *Preventing reading difficulties in young children.* Washington, DC: National Academy Press.

Reading Methods Textbooks

If you want additional instructional ideas or more complete descriptions of the strategies and activities in this book, or if you want thorough lists of topical references, then you should consult a reading methods text. Two from the publisher of this book are:

Reutzel, D. R., & Cooter, R. B. (2004). *Teaching children to read: Putting the pieces together (4th ed.).* Upper Saddle River, NJ: Pearson/Merrill/Prentice Hall.

Tompkins, G. E. (2006). *Literacy for the 21st century: A balanced approach.* Upper Saddle River, NJ: Pearson/Merrill/Prentice Hall.

Other Books on Teaching Reading

The brief companion document to the *Report of the National Reading Panel* is:

Armbuster, B. B., Lehr, F., & Osborn, J. (2001). *Put reading first: The research building blocks for teaching children to read: Kindergarten through Grade 3.* Washington DC: National Insitute of Child Health and Human Development/U.S. Department of Education/National Institute of Literacy.

Books that focus on specific topics in reading instruction are excellent sources of instructional ideas, such as:

Adams, M. J., Foorman, B. R., Lundberg, I., & Beeler, T. (1999). *Phonemic awareness in young children: A classroom curriculum.* Baltimore: Paul Brookes.

Bear, D. R., Invernizzi, M., Templeton, S., & Johnston, F. (2004). *Words their way: Word study for phonics, vocabulary, and spelling instruction (3rd ed.).* Upper Saddle River, NJ: Pearson/Merrill/Prentice Hall.

Journal Articles

Articles about reading instruction appear in many journals. For elementary reading instruction, two journals from the International Reading Association are essential reading: *Reading Research Quarterly,* which publishes research articles and reviews; and *The Reading Teacher,* with articles focusing on instruction, written for classroom practitioners. Each issue has many classroom teaching ideas to consider. For example, the May 2005 issue of *The Reading Teacher* had very good articles on reading fluency (Hudson, Lane, and Pullen) and morphemic analysis (Mountain).

Appendixes

Appendix A

Graded Word Lists

Student Name _____ **Highest instructional level (2w)** _____

A (PP)	**B** (P)	**C** (1.0)	**D** (2.0)
_____ the	_____ come	_____ today	_____ biggest
_____ am	_____ you	_____ does	_____ where
_____ get	_____ went	_____ three	_____ yourself
_____ is	_____ him	_____ from	_____ those
_____ and	_____ two	_____ under	_____ before
_____ here	_____ then	_____ began	_____ things
_____ see	_____ know	_____ name	_____ stopped
_____ not	_____ around	_____ there	_____ place
_____ can	_____ pet	_____ could	_____ always
_____ will	_____ house	_____ again	_____ everyone

E (3.0)	**F** (4.0)	**G** (5.0)	**H** (6.0)
_____ morning	_____ important	_____ because	_____ aircraft
_____ since	_____ airport	_____ bridge	_____ necessary
_____ together	_____ through	_____ microscope	_____ argument
_____ begin	_____ fifteen	_____ curious	_____ chemical
_____ which	_____ information	_____ estimation	_____ representative
_____ near	_____ ocean	_____ reliable	_____ terminal
_____ should	_____ preview	_____ government	_____ apology
_____ yesterday	_____ laughter	_____ business	_____ instruction
_____ eight	_____ preparation	_____ direction	_____ evidence
_____ remember	_____ building	_____ avenue	_____ consideration

From Lois A. Bader, *Bader Reading and Language Inventory* (3rd ed.), p. 13. Columbus, OH: Merrill/Prentice Hall, 1998. Reprinted with permission.

Appendix B

Scoring Sheet for Graded Word Lists

Student Name _Valerie_ **Highest instructional level (2w)** _1_
Grade: 1

A (PP)	**B** (P)	**C** (1.0)	**D** (2.0)
✓ the	✓ come	✓ today	*BAGGEST* ___ biggest *C*
✓ am	✓ you	✓ does	✓ where
✓ get	✓ went	✓ three	✓ yourself
✓ is	*HIT* ___ him *C*	✓ from	✓✓ those
✓ and	✓ two	(under)	✓ before
✓ here	✓ then	✓ began	✓ things
✓ see	*KA-NO‾* ___ know	✓ name	*STEPPED* ___ stopped
✓✓ not	✓✓ around	✓ there	✓✓ place
✓ can	✓ pet	*COLD* ___ could	(always)
✓ will	✓ house	✓ again	*AIRYONE* ___ everyone

✓ CORRECT   ✓✓ HESITATES   C SELF-CORRECTION
(circle) COULDN'T SAY

E (3.0)	**F** (4.0)	**G** (5.0)	**H** (6.0)
___ morning	___ important	___ because	___ aircraft
___ since	___ airport	___ bridge	___ necessary
___ together	___ through	___ microscope	___ argument
___ begin	___ fifteen	___ curious	___ chemical
___ which	___ information	___ estimation	___ representative
___ near	___ ocean	___ reliable	___ terminal
___ should	___ preview	___ government	___ apology
___ yesterday	___ laughter	___ business	___ instruction
___ eight	___ preparation	___ direction	___ evidence
___ remember	___ building	___ avenue	___ consideration

Appendix C

Graded Reading Passage—Grade 1

Tony and the Flower Shop

Tony lived in a big city. He ran a flower shop. Tony loved his flowers, for the flowers did not make any noise. Tony loved peace and quiet.

The city where Tony lived was noisy. The buses, trucks, and cars were very noisy. He did not like the noise of the city.

Without the quiet Tony found in the flower shop, he would have moved from the city. The flower shop was his only reason for staying in the city.

From Lois A. Bader, *Reader's Passages to Accompany Bader Reading and Language Inventory* (3rd ed.), p. 8. Columbus, OH: Merrill/Prentice Hall, 1998. Reprinted with permission.

Appendix D

Graded Reading Passage—Grade 6

Constellations

People all over the world have looked at the stars and have seen patterns that reminded them of everyday things. A group of stars that forms such a pattern is a constellation. A constellation lies within a definite region of the sky. By knowing the positions of the constellations, one can locate stars, planets, comets, and other galaxies. There are eighty-eight officially recognized constellations.

Many of the ancient names for certain constellations are still used today, though the things they were named for are no longer a part of our everday experiences.

Almost anyone who grew up in the Northern Hemisphere can point out the Little Dipper. The Little Dipper is part of the constellation Ursa Minor, which means Little Bear.

Ursa Minor appears to circle the North Star. It is visible all year long. Some groups of stars are only visible during certain seasons of the year.

There are twelve seasonal constellations that are especially important because the sun and the moon always rise within one of their patterns. These are the constellations of the Zodiac.

Constellations are used in ship and airplane navigation. Astronauts use them to help orient spacecraft.

From Lois A. Bader, *Reader's Passages to Accompany Bader Reading and Language Inventory* (3rd ed.), p. 23. Columbus, OH: Merrill/Prentice Hall, 1998. Reprinted with permission.

Appendix E

Scoring System for Oral Reading Miscue Analysis

Substitution and mispronunciations
Underline and write the student's response above the word

Example: they <u>will</u> go to principal's office
(above "will": shall)

Repeated word
Underline and write "R" above the word or phrase that was repeated

Example: Fred decided to go <u>to the movies.</u>
(above "to the movies": R)

Insertions
Write the word the student inserted with a caret

Example: the ^big bear
(above caret: big)

Omissions
Circle the word omitted

Example: and so the (grumpy) giant walked

Words provided by the person giving the test
Underline the word and write T above it

Example: was so heavy it took three <u>sailors</u> to lift it
(above "sailors": T)

Self-corrections by the student
Underline the word, write the word the student said first, then write a C

Example: the <u>terrible</u> storm destroyed
(above "terrible": terrific C)

Appendix F

Scoring Sheet—Graded Reading Passage

Student's Name _____Debbie_____ **Date** _11/21/06_

Passage Level: 3

JAMES' CUT

It was after lunch when James cut his finger on the playground. He was bleeding

    HURTING

and <u>he hurt</u> a little too.

                                R

He went inside to find his teacher. He showed her his <u>cut finger</u> and asked for

   R

a Band-Aid. <u>She</u> looked at it and said, "Well, it's not too bad, James. I think we should

               You

wash it before <u>we</u> bandage it, don't you" James did not want it washed because he

                                      ACT

thought it would sting. But he was afraid to tell Miss Smith. He just <u>acted</u> brave.

                 a   **WHEN**

When it was washed <u>and</u> bandaged, he thanked Miss Smith. <u>Then</u> he rushed

out to the playground to show everyone his shiny new bandage.

Passage from Lois A. Bader, *Reader's Passages to Accompany Bader Reading and Language Inventory* (3rd ed.), p. 13. Columbus, OH: Merrill/Prentice Hall, 1998. Reprinted with permission.

Appendix G

Diagrams of Expository Text Structures

Cause and Effect

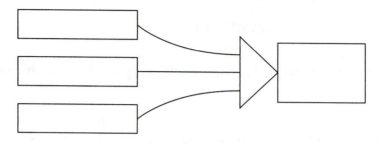

Problem and Solution

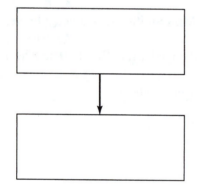

Comparison/Contrast

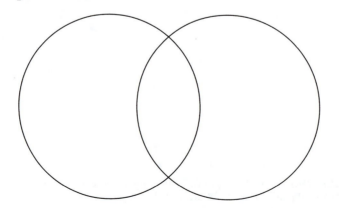

Sequence

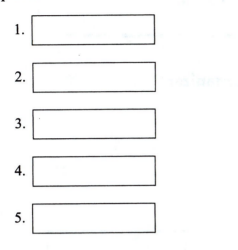

1.

2.

3.

4.

5.

Description

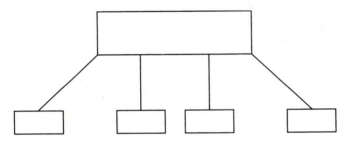

Appendix H

Graphic Organizer

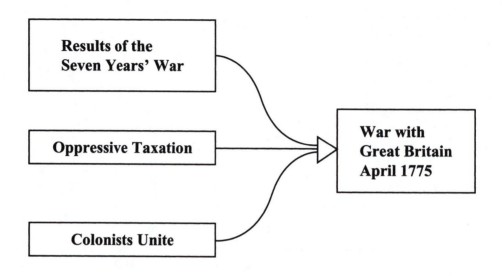

Appendix I

Study Guide Based on Text Structure

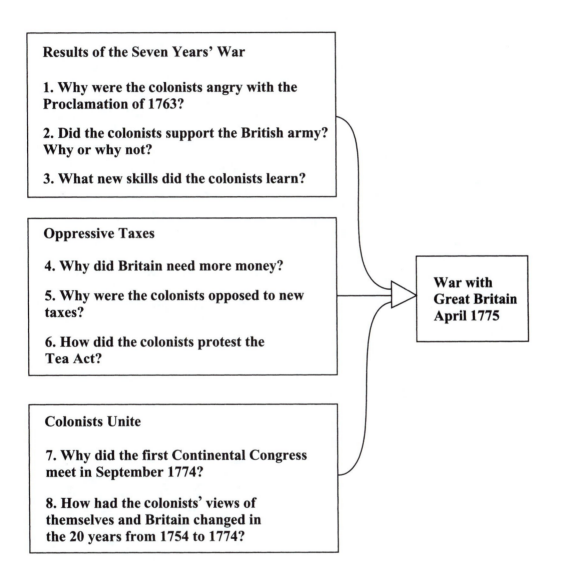

Results of the Seven Years' War

1. Why were the colonists angry with the Proclamation of 1763?

2. Did the colonists support the British army? Why or why not?

3. What new skills did the colonists learn?

Oppressive Taxes

4. Why did Britain need more money?

5. Why were the colonists opposed to new taxes?

6. How did the colonists protest the Tea Act?

Colonists Unite

7. Why did the first Continental Congress meet in September 1774?

8. How had the colonists' views of themselves and Britain changed in the 20 years from 1754 to 1774?

War with Great Britain April 1775

Index